From cosy family delights to lo..g, ...y, ... nights, from fragmented existences to rebuilding life anew as a couple or bravely solo, the letters are a tapestry of what is most integral to the soul – the necessity to belong, to a person, a family created or reconstructed, a city, oneself – and to carry forward the sacred gift of memory with grace and compassion.

– Pallavi Narayan, PhD
Co-editor of *Singapore at Home: Life across Lines*
and author of *Pamuk's Istanbul: The Self and the City*

Heartfelt love letters that will resonate, whether you're still on that universal quest for a soulmate, or your life has already been made almost complete.

– Koh Buck Song
Author, poet and brand adviser

The collection tells the inner feelings of these amazing individuals who have experienced love, romance, heartbreak, loss, and grief. *Letter to My Partner* feels like taking a glimpse inside someone's heart – so intimate, raw and relatable. An inspiring read that would make you smile and cry, and a reminder that while your love story may take you to places you've never expected, in the end, we're all the better because of it.

– Violet Lim
CEO & Co-Founder, Lunch Actually

Letter to my Partner

Letter to my Partner

*Words of love and
perspectives of marriage*

EDITED BY FELIX CHEONG

Marshall Cavendish
Editions

Text © individual contributors as credited in each work
© 2022 Marshall Cavendish International (Asia) Private Limited

Published in 2022 by Marshall Cavendish Editions
An imprint of Marshall Cavendish International

A member of the
Times Publishing Group

Other Marshall Cavendish Offices:
Marshall Cavendish Corporation, 800 Westchester Ave, Suite N-641, Rye Brook,
NY 10573, USA • Marshall Cavendish International (Thailand) Co Ltd, 253 Asoke,
16th Floor, Sukhumvit 21 Road, Klongtoey Nua, Wattana, Bangkok 10110, Thailand
• Marshall Cavendish (Malaysia) Sdn Bhd, Times Subang, Lot 46, Subang Hi-Tech
Industrial Park, Batu Tiga, 40000 Shah Alam, Selangor Darul Ehsan, Malaysia

Marshall Cavendish is a registered trademark of Times Publishing Limited

National Library Board, Singapore Cataloguing-in-Publication Data

Name(s): Cheong, Felix, editor.
Title: Letter to my partner : words of love and perspectives of marriage / edited by Felix
   Cheong.
Description: Singapore : Marshall Cavendish Editions, 2022.
Identifier(s): ISBN 978-981-5009-30-9 (paperback)
Subject(s): LCSH: Spouses--Correspondence. | Marriage. | Love.
Classification: DDC 306.872--dc23

Printed in Singapore

Cover design by Adithi Khandadai

Contents

Foreword

Felix Cheong

What is hardest to talk about is always what is up close and too personal. There is too much at stake, too little to gain from candour. Not forgetting you would need distance and time apart for a sense of perspective.

Which is why *Letter to My Partner*, the fifth in our *Letter* series, has been the most challenging for me as editor. For the previous three volumes (*Son, Mother and Father*), almost every contributor I had approached had agreed readily. Words were forthcoming when written at arm's length, when the pen did not need to dip – or perhaps stab – deep into the heart.

For this anthology, I had contacted more than 40 people. One after another, they declined: It is too painful, too shameful, they told me. There are things my partner does not want me to reveal. There are things about me I do not want my partner to know.

Of course, I understood. I myself would have hesitated to commit private words to such a public letter. It would have taken courage – and much handwringing – to talk about my

previous marriage, the spouse I had once failed. It would have taken courage – and much beating of the breast – to talk to my current spouse, of the times I had failed her.

Which is why these 18 brave souls who eventually agreed to contribute a letter to their partner (former or current) must be applauded for their heartfelt words, often confessional and still so raw they hurt.

Theirs is a measure of bonds forged over trying circumstances, of relationships long at rest or still in motion. Theirs is a sizing up of love in all its phases, from first flush to last gasp, through the years of giving-ins and misgivings, and all the pit-stops in-between that start and stall.

Here is what needs to be said, and I do hope you will be inspired to write to your partner after reading their letters.

FELIX CHEONG is the author of 21 books, including six volumes of poetry, a trilogy of satirical flash fiction and seven children's picture books. His works have been nominated for the prestigious Frank O'Connor Award and the Singapore Literature Prize. His latest work is *Sprawl*, a graphic novel in collaboration with Malaysian artist Arif Rafhan.

Conferred the Young Artist Award in 2000, Felix holds a Masters in Creative Writing and is currently a university adjunct lecturer with the National University of Singapore, University of Newcastle, Murdoch University and Curtin University.

An Escalator Instead of a Lift

Jon Gresham

Dear Darling,

What if I had caught the lift instead of the escalator?

I was never looking for a wife. I did not want a wife. At that time, I just wanted the world's greatest corporate restructuring plan to succeed.

During the early years of the 21st century, I was in Jakarta trying to persuade the Indonesian press, the government and businesses that corporate restructuring was the best thing since *nasi goreng*.

I did this by taking influencers up four escalators to a bento set lunch every Monday for a couple of months at Plaza Senayan, a high-end shopping mall in Central Jakarta. At the restaurant on the top floor, I chatted with editors, ministerial advisors and bankers about the traffic, global politics and the restructuring. Those were tense days, tainted by America's lust for war in Iraq, the horror of the recent Bali bombings, and the fear a similar carnage would occur in Jakarta.

On my first bento lunch as I rode the escalator to the third floor, I spotted you in a perfume shop, with your hair up, stacking the shelves with little white boxes of Chanel No 5. From a distance, we made eye contact and smiled at the same time. In my diary, I wrote: "Creditors getting screwed on restructuring. Grinned at girl in perfume shop. Black dress. Slim. Wide smile. Funny. Bought Hugo Boss Dark Blue. Stank. Listened to The Jam's *Monday* on iPod over and over again."

I bought T-shirts from the shop next door, ties and shirts from the tailor opposite. It took me about 12 rides on the escalator before I found the courage to enter the perfume shop and speak to you. After that first visit, I returned the next week and purchased a bottle of Drakkar Noir. The following week, Fahrenheit. The week after that, L'Eau D'Issey, Guerlain, and Elizabeth Taylor's Passion. You thought they were for a wife I never had. You thought I was some married guy wanting to have a bit on the side. I gave these bottles of perfume to my mother and sister.

I asked you out and we drank orange juice in the food court. You liked Westlife, A-ha, Michael Learns to Rock, *Friends*, Tiffany's, Audrey Hepburn and Scooby Doo. You thought I had a wife and kids. The only family I had, in fact, was a folder full of spreadsheets and legal agreements.

A month later, we went on our first date. We watched one of the worst movies I have ever seen: *The Core* – about a team of scientists drilling to the centre of the earth to save the human race. We had to be chaperoned, so you brought along seven friends.

At that time, you were so thin I thought you were ill. When I first tried to hold your hand, I could have held your wrist in a circle made between the tips of my trigger finger and thumb. Like making an okay sign to feel your pulse. Your softness.

We connected, though we came from different worlds. To get to work, you had to take multiple bus trips from your kampung, off Jalan Mohammed Kahfi, across Jakarta – that usually took two-and-a-half hours or more. For me, it took just an hour for my driver to take me in a limo from the Shangri-La Hotel to World Trade Centre on Sudirman.

My work in Jakarta soon ended and I returned to the desolate streets of Singapore in the grip of SARS. We lost contact – it was just too hard to stay in touch. Several months later, I was surprised to receive your text. You cracked a joke about brushing your teeth. I cannot remember the details; just that it was really funny and it brightened my evening.

Then we lost touch again. As always, I was consumed by work. My personal life only had room – and time – for street photography and watching English Premier League football. I could not commit to anyone. Those were the days of "shock and awe" when the US invaded Iraq. I was appalled at the Americans' headlong rush into an illegal and irrational war. Love was the furthest thing from my mind.

You rang me six months later to say a man, someone who made couches, had asked you to marry him. I did not know what to say. But you asked me how you could say no. I was the worst possible person to consult on such matters. I did not want to get involved because it was none of my business.

Soon after, you rang again to tell me you were getting married to this American furniture manufacturer. His dowry included a lounge set and dining table. Three days before the wedding, you asked if you could visit me in Singapore, to stay for a while, get yourself together because you did not want to marry the American. I was speechless.

The importance of that moment hit me in the face. Whatever answer I gave would swing our lives one way or the other. I said yes. I rang your uncle and told him the wedding was off. Funnily, he mistook me for your husband-to-be and chatted about bedframes. After multiple clarifications, you finally arrived in Singapore – and have never left.

When you first arrived at my place at Kim Yam Road, I remember you wore a sky-blue velour tracksuit. You were afraid the American was searching for you here. His lawyer had once shown up at your family home in Jakarta. You were so afraid you would not dare to walk to Cold Storage on your own. Eventually, you conquered your fear of the mean streets around River Valley Road.

I remember asking your father's permission to marry you at your family home. He was a batik designer and factory owner from Pekalongan, who had lost his business to an unscrupulous partner. He was so shy and quiet. He whispered to your uncle, who translated the "yes" for me. Your mother laughed and told me tales of her childhood watching *wayang kulit* cast across large linen sheets in an open field, illuminated by the light from coconut oil lamps.

Do you remember our two weddings? The first was in Jakarta, where we dressed like a Javanese prince and princess, and you cried as we exchanged our vows – I was so worried you were having second thoughts. My father danced to *dangdut* and kept sitting on his kris. Then we were off to Bali and the Istana at Uluwatu, with cliffs overlooking the vast Indian Ocean. Fishing boats far out on the horizon and surfers below. Do you remember the clouds rolling in at dawn and the orchids in the infinity pool, Laras' sulking, and how you stole the night with your beauty and wedding speech?

Seventeen years and 15kg later, I emerge as the ultimate beneficiary of our time together. So many memories, and so many things to be thankful for.

Thank you for the chicken and broccoli lasagne, the spinach chocolate chip cookies and the hummus. Thank you for the meerkat impersonations and tom yum kung, your sweet corn patties, roast lamb and how you once made roast beef on the day I had to visit the dentist.

I love it when you wash your hair with an egg. I do not really mind if you detest cricket. I do not mind if your hair is grey. I do not mind if you wear a hijab, but know I am likely to get into a fight if you wear it in Australia and someone abuses you.

I knew you had a good sense of humour when, after I had sprinkled myself with talcum powder, you told me I looked like a Dunkin' Donut. I told you I used to be as thin as you. You laughed, handed me some more chocolate chip and peanut butter cookies and gave me the same piece of advice you had once given me: "Be like a waterfall. Go with the flow. Just go with the flow."

You told me when I am doing my writing, my mouth wiggles, squirms and pouts in concentration. You wrote in my diary that when I was a teen, I looked like Nick Jonas. When you get annoyed, you grunt a little like Marge Simpson, roll your eyes and say: "Oh, honey." You do not get what I write – that is okay. You are not alone.

Do you remember when we jogged down Mount Faber? I jumped on your back and you twisted and broke your ankle in the gutter because I was fooling round. I apologise, though it was nice pushing you around in a wheelchair for four months. God, you are good to put up with me!

Do you remember our worst day, when you nearly died? During the night, you had stomach cramps, so the next morning we went to see the doctor. You were so pale. There was blood. This general practitioner congratulated you on your pregnancy; we were joyful – for a while. She sent us to the Paragon to see a gynaecologist, who had a worried look after the ultrasound scan. I had never heard of ectopic pregnancies before. She booked you immediately for emergency surgery at Mount Elizabeth Hospital. I felt like I was somewhere else when she told me the percentage probability you could die. We were told to expect plus one, and then minus one – all in the space of three hours. We grieved for that loss in quietness and solitude. We tried and we tried again. Years of pills and jabs, sacks, linings and mucus. We grieved for more of those lost. Those who never existed. I did not know what else to do, but you kept going, with courage and resilience. I remember that strength – it was what kept us going.

Five years later, there is joy. Thanks to you and the gynaecologist, we have Sophia. Sophia the fearless delight. Our bundle of eccentric happiness. The rejector of princesses whose role models are Spider Gwen, Wednesday Addams, Bad Jelly the Witch…and above all, you. Thank you for

Sophia and doing the hard yards, for being a creative person and stitching together the "Sam-I-am", Hungry Caterpillar and Easter Bunny costumes.

Do you remember when you nearly died again? Two years ago, your gall bladder nearly exploded. You shivered and went into shock, with your body jolting and your legs in spasm. It reminded me of the time my mother had a fit from encephalitis. She stood on all fours on her bed, saliva frothing at the mouth, staring at me without any sign of recognition. I called an ambulance and left Sophia with the next-door neighbours. Your gall stones were the size of peas and you stayed in hospital for 10 days while I took care of Sophia by myself. We ate yoghurt and cheese, banana and Nutella the whole time. You came home and told me off for not cleaning the kitchen properly and not buying enough groceries.

I have never been as near to dying as you. Unless you count how close I was to catching a lift rather than an escalator nearly 20 years ago at Plaza Senayan.

How beautiful you are, Darling. Even the soles of your feet are soft. Behind your shyness, your nose goes red in winter. Remember Paris in winter? You looked so much cooler in your shades than the Easter Island statue in the Louvre. And remember the early morning on the junk cruise on Ha Long Bay? Wrapped in your fur-lined hoodie, you looked like a koala but with a dash of red at the tip of your nose.

Of course, you know all this. You were there. But I am retelling it now to remind ourselves how we came to be. You are calm and elegant. Prettier now than ever, even as we go grey together. You are funny, intelligent, down to earth and my best friend. I remain proud and honoured to be married to you. I thank you for your kindness and patience, for making your daughter and me happy.

And for smiling that day when I took the escalator instead of the lift.

Lots of love
Jon

JON GRESHAM is the author of the short story collection *We Rose Up Slowly* (Math Paper Press, 2015, 2nd edition) and co-editor with Elizabeth Tan of *In This Desert There Were Seeds* (Ethos Books and Margaret River Press, 2019). His writing has appeared in various publications, including *The Best Asian Short Stories 2020* (Kitaab 2020) and *Best Singaporean Short Stories 1* (Epigram Books 2020). His story, "The Visit", was shortlisted for the 2020 Short Fiction/ Essex University Prize. He helps run the Asia Creative Writing Programme, a collaboration between the National Arts Council and Nanyang Technological University. He is a co-founder of Sing Lit Station.

Getting to Know You[1]

Donna Tang

I have not seen you in two weeks when I step out of the Kuala Lumpur International Airport, and then I do. Common wisdom says it is too soon for us to holiday together, but one of the benefits of having been through heartbreak and divorces is that the rules do not apply anymore.

When I slip into your car, I am suddenly shy. I want to place a hand on your knee, but instead muse out of the window that the sun looks different here. We are now in the land where you and your wife had loved each other, cupped your hands around the flame, then blew it out. When you were in Singapore, your past was just a story, like something forwarded on the Internet. But here, the signboards are in another language, and her iPhone is still paired to the car sound system, her name in the menu like the most natural thing. I feel displaced, misplaced.

Throughout our few months dating, I have been a timid woodland animal, slow to warm up and quick to dart away.

1 First published in the Jan 2021 issue of www.qlrs.com

I sniff the air now, writing anxiety in it with my quivering nose. You sense this and, in your patient planning voice, begin to detail the things we could do. I relax a little into your orderliness, into the man I know back home.

Then, you are almost shy when you ask if you can show me your hometown. We have a nice hotel booked in the city, replete with stars and spas, and I am a city girl. I turn to look at you as if arriving for the first time, and you take your eyes off the highway to receive me, your held breath a question mark. Yes, I say, I would love that, and your face breaks open with such delight my heart swells.

You are like a child now, chattering nonstop with a surprise you can barely contain. Historically, the tin-rich Klang Valley had once sparked a war between Rajas, and Klang itself has been both the royal seat of power and state capital of Selangor. Today, it still boasts Malaysia's biggest seaport but is more popularly known for being the birthplace of *bak kut teh* – Chinese pork rib soup.

Entering Klang Old Town, sooty shophouses line the roads like decaying teeth, creeping plants cleaving roofs and faces. Broken windows, cracked tail-lights, drains exposed like something impolite, like an old lady's blouse falling open. Skeletons of buildings, abandoned midway through construction, stand starkly etched against the sky. The pavements have erupted and trash floats in Klang River – but you see none of this. Watching you spill over with buzzy, childlike pride, I understand what it would be like to be loved by you, flaws and all.

You indicate landmarks – the Sultan's palace, the golden-domed Pasar Jawa Mosque – but it is the ones of sentimental instead of tourist value that I learn carefully. There is the police station, striped blue-and-white; here, the Victorian-style fire station. Over there, the cake shop that made every one of your childhood birthday cakes. And here is your favourite *bak kut teh* shop, in a town full of *bak kut teh* shops, and we park by the road so I can try some.

I open the car door and pause. The car tips dangerously towards the open drain; there is a rusty old washing machine in it someone has left for dead. I bury my bag under the seat when you are not looking and shut the door.

I tail you into the shop; the gap-toothed proprietor greets you like family. You introduce me as your friend from Singapore, and that is as far as my Hokkien carries me, so I do not know if the pride in your voice is for me, or for what I am about to eat. The old man stands a little longer at our table appraising me, one leg up, cracked sole of a foot on the side of a knee. His tongue twiddles a gold tooth while I blow on a spoonful of the thick herbal broth. It is complex, savoury, smooth. Thick from hours of brewing, it is at once rich, and floral-sweet from Chinese herbs. It is nothing like the thin, pale version I get back home. I swallow, grin – you beam and pull fork-tender pork ribs out of the soup for me. I take a square photo of the meal – and the old man beams, brings extra fried shallots to sprinkle on my rice.

Wherever you are in the world, an Instagram is worth 10,000 words.

We drive around town, and I catch glimpses of you everywhere. There you are, age two, arriving from Canada in your father's hot muggy hometown, in your beautiful blonde mother's arms. Age five, hair lit as bright as curry, running from house to house along your grandfather's road, the row of identical red-and-pink bungalows, one for each family, everyone thrilled to see you.

We stop for artisanal coffee in an old shophouse-turned-hipster-cafe, and I spot you, age seven, pointing out the backpack you want, outside the store two doors away that still sells school uniforms and supplies. Age eleven, panic-cycling home from school, through the under-the-bridge darkness where bullies hide.

Fifteen, strategically positioned for a good view of the local girls' school at the *roti canai* shop opposite, where we shred fluffy Indian crepes and I lick curry off my fingers. Seventeen, becoming the man of the house when your father dies suddenly, leaving your mother five children and a lifetime of longing.

You, working and shielding younger siblings from trouble, while still in school yourself; building a career, driving hours to and from the city to lay your head down close to family every night. You, only a year ago, bracing for divorce, making painful arrangements for your mother's funeral rites.

Everywhere we go, you are greeted with so much love it spills over to this stranger as well. The lady who makes your favourite sticky pork chop rice presses a massive bottle of peanut cookies into my hands. Old friends and their elderly parents call out to you from across narrow streets: "Hey, *ang moh*, how long are you back from Singapore for?"

The brown river that oozes through the town is lined with weeping willows. At low tide, it smells of salt and shit. I do not know if I could call Klang home; but you, you I could.

DONNA TANG is a former lifestyle editor, who is currently pursuing an MA Creative Writing. Her poetry and prose have been featured in anthologies such as *The Best Asian Short Stories*, *Meridian: The APWT Drunken Boat Anthology of New Writing*, and the *Quarterly Literary Review Singapore*. She is interested in memory and identity-construction, and is working on her first novel.

Far, Far Beyond the Stars

Hamish Brown

My dearest Lena,

As I write this, it strikes me in all the time I have known you and in all the years we have been together, from you being a casual friend to now my beloved wife, I have never actually written a letter to you, ever.

I am both amused and, frankly, rather embarrassed by this.

The magnificent artistry of eloquent prose and wit that can magnify emotion and be immortalised in words to be savoured, like a fine wine, when they are read again, is certainly something to be cherished and treasured like a family heirloom.

Frankly, I was a little disappointed at myself to admit this was down to neglect, in the face of work commitments and, well, admittedly taking you for granted. For this, please let me say how sorry I am.

For everything that I am today could not have been, without your steadfast support and belief in my wildest of dreams. So, here it goes.

***

As I write this, I am looking at the magnificent view that greets us every morning from our villa up on Bophut Hill here in Koh Samui, where we have called home the past eight years. This has always been my dream: To be able to retire by the time I am 50 and watch sunrises and sunsets across the Gulf of Thailand. To dine on fresh seafood and knock back an exquisite single malt with the love of my life and not have a care in the world.

But dreams remain dreams, unless action is taken to manifest them and that is where the first of my many thanks to you must start.

They say that opposites attract. Looking at us, two more diametrically opposed poles could not be more evident.

You were petite and sweet like a hummingbird, highly focused on goals but with a fierce determination. You loved the classical arts and hobnobbed with society's elites as the nature of your job at the British High Council entailed. You dazzled among your circle of friends like a blinding beacon of light, drawing everyone to your warmth and personable qualities effortlessly and easily.

And here I was, a national broadcaster on morning radio on weekdays, juggling creative director duties with my own events management company in the highly competitive field of corporate and commercial entertainment. You could say we were the real-life equivalent of that Disney movie, *Lady and The Tramp*.

I remember in later years, you confided in me how your friends were worried you might be making a grave mistake with me as your choice of partner. I think one of them summed it up in the best Singapore style ever: "You sure or not?"

I am so glad you never wavered from your conviction. Somehow, you saw something in this tramp that made you take a leap of faith. For that, I give thanks every day.

We had both been through a previous marriage, so our wedding vows, exchanged on a small balcony extension near the walkway at Labrador Park overlooking the shoreline and the flora and fauna of Singapore's West Coast, was our version of the Hollywood perfect ending. But really, that was just the start of our adventure.

I want to thank you for wanting to focus on celebrating us. No huge banquet dinner hall filled with unfamiliar faces; just a small group of family and very close friends. You made sure conventions went out the window, even down to wanting to drive to our luncheon celebration on your own. Thankfully, you did not, in the end, much to everyone's relief, mine the most. But it does make for pleasant and hilarious moments to reminisce and toast to with each glorious year.

People have asked me: "What made me realise she was *the one*?" I always tell them the same thing. When you are able to have scintillating conversations about a mutual interest like cinema, for instance, not just the stories but the intricacies behind its making, or discuss which movie or musical songs are the most inspirational, the exhilaration lingers and endures, like a blanket that feels at once warm, safe and perfectly right.

Truth be told, when I found out you were equally fascinated as I was to watch documentaries of how movies were made, I knew, right there and then, that you were a keeper. There was no question. It felt like winning the lottery. How often does anyone get that sort of feeling? Well, in my case, it is every time a movie we both love ends, and we seek out the special making-of extras on the disc to pour over, fascinated by the behind-the-scene magic.

Enjoying a wonderful movie is only half the experience, of course, if one does not have mouthwatering snacks to accompany the filmic experience. What is better is making one's own culinary delights and enjoying it as a couple – that would be heaven on earth.

There was just one small problem: I was an absolute washout in the kitchen.

I think a bit of context is required at this point.

As you know, I grew up with two much older sisters. So, I had not one, but three mothers, in a manner of speaking. Being the baby of the family, the always ravenous me was in and out of the kitchen constantly, looking for food. I was a tad curious how Mum made those wonderful Eurasian dishes. But every time I attempted to "help" in the kitchen, the oestrogen squad would quickly bundle me out as I would inadvertently drop ingredients or break some cutlery through carelessness or clumsiness. I was like a bull in a china shop, and then some, for I was always waiting to swipe scoops of whatever was cooking at that moment.

Anyway, all this meant that cooking was simply a skill

too far for me. That is, until you showed me just how wonderful cooking could be and not the nightmare I had envisioned: Water splashing and hot oil popping at every single moment. The day you helped me make the perfect scrambled eggs, just the way you like them, creamy and slightly runny, was truly a red-letter day for me. Admittedly, I had been pouring over many hours of Gordon Ramsey's YouTube videos and going over it in my head many times over – even while I was cooking!

Through it all, you were patiently by my side, holding my hand and showing me there was nothing to fear in this brave new adventure. You also taught me how not to lose my cool when things in the pan sizzle and flame. Slowly, I graduated from scrambled eggs to doing steak the way you like it – well done – and the way I like mine, medium, with just that right touch of glorious red to bring out the hunter in me.

I guess our love for similar things is another reason how much of a guiding force you are in my life. A gentle life teacher, but very effective in imparting sacred knowledge that if one wants something bad enough, one has to put one's mind and energy to it to make it happen. I would also like to take this opportunity to give a shout-out to acclaimed writer, novelist and dear friend, Neil Gaiman, for my next big life lesson, courtesy of my wife.

It was Neil's 50th birthday in November 2010. You and Neil were – and still are – very close friends, as you had brought him to Singapore for the first time when you were working at the British Council years ago. You have remained in close contact with him since.

I remember you coming home one day and telling me

you had received an email from him, an invitation to his 50th birthday. What an incredible honour. Neil was pretty much literary royalty, and this was akin to being invited to Buckingham Palace by the Queen herself.

There was just one tiny problem.

As luck would have it, the date clashed with a conference event you were running in Kuala Lumpur. Although it was on the last day of the conference, and his birthday was to be celebrated in New Orleans the next day, it was still a nightmare of managing flight connections.

Despite the benefit of being a day ahead in time zone, doing this trip meant leaving the running of the conference in the capable hands of your colleagues, catching the last flight from KL back to Singapore at midnight, then an early flight at 7am, with layovers in Tokyo and Houston, followed by a final transfer to a domestic carrier that would take us to Louis Armstrong Airport in New Orleans.

This plan of the literal jet-set also meant razor-thin transfer windows. If just one of our flights was delayed by an hour, we would probably not be able to make it. But I forgot I was speaking to "she who never gives up and never says 'not possible if it can be done somehow'".

I remember one leg was slightly less than an hour in a huge airport; this meant we had to run at top speed to catch the connecting flight and pray to the gods our baggage would make it as fast as we did. This also meant having very little to practically no sleep after landing in Singapore from KL, switching bags and making sure I had packed everything.

How you managed to find all the connecting flights and

pull it off spectacularly, still has me in amazement to this day. Somehow, with your attention to detail and sheer force of will and fierce belief in the power of good karma, the whole trip was made without incident or delay.

We arrived with an hour and a half to spare, just enough time to shower and freshen up for an incredible birthday bash which boasted a who's who of the literary gods and movie-making world. The co-scriptwriter of *Pulp Fiction*, Roger Avery, was there, as were a few American film stars. British comedy legend Lenny Henry was gliding through the crowd, which also included author and humorist John Hodgeman.

How we partied. We hobnobbed with the Hollywood "in-crowd" and we were even acknowledged by Neil as the guests who had flown the furthest to attend his birthday bash. This was a moment I will never forget – just one of many memories we could not have made without your tenacity to run with an idea and see it from start to finish. Those moments – and may there be many more – are all because of you, my magnificent North Star.

As we travel life's journey together, the only thing that matters more to me than all the best loved movies in the world, is to say thank you. A billion times over, and it would still not be enough.

All my love and all my thanks. To the moon and back and far, far beyond the stars.

Just Me.

HAMISH BROWN has over 40 years of experience as a radio presenter/producer, show host and moderator. He is also a well-known professional voice artiste for radio, TV commercials and documentaries that are beamed across Asia. In 1990, he founded Journey Promotions Pte Ltd together with some friends and was its creative director and partner until he left and retired.

In his free time, Hamish loves cooking and has written online reviews for *Appetite Asia*. He also enjoys watching movies and was a director and curator for the 2010 Singapore International Film Festival.

He is now happily retired in Thailand with his wife Lena.

Letter to My Angel aka
(I Don't Say) Thank You (Enough)

Ning Cai

To my dearest Angel,

Thank you
for being so brave and relentless
taking your chances with
a reckless daydreamer
who once believed herself
forever young, untouchable
easy to fall in love with
but impossible
to stay in love with
fated for a lonely life
a wandering gypsy
without roots
chasing the winds
just following the gigs wherever
opportunity and ambition took her
until you came along

and discovered my secret
(this girl's a walking contradiction –
living large and dying inside)
and despite all odds
our staggering differences;
clash of love languages
my fears and insecurities
my selfishness and immaturity
my reservations about loving
someone on the spectrum
practical, non-romantic
but you became
my very definition
of home

Thank you
for telling me I'm wrong
when I'm too stubborn to
open my shrouded eyes
to other ways of seeing;
for calling me out
on my own damning lies
all the bullshit I tell myself
and almost believed in;
for showing me it's okay
to not always be okay
when memory leads me
a shackled prisoner
down inky shadows
of dark twisted spaces;

for always being truthful
even when you and I/ we
are hurting (bleeding)
our wounded hearts heavy;
for lighting up my world –
a raging wildfire
you stop my stumble
through dark emptiness
scorching embers of
calescent star stuff;
for a lifetime of
inspiration through action
like keeping your promise
to break bad habits
extinguishing them
out of your life
forever;
and last but not least
for your vow (on the
first day of summer)
of making your home
in my heart: always

Thank you
for taking these
little pieces of me
a thousand shards
untouched
buried in secret
never seeing the light

your bare feet
anchored
in the depths of my very core
where you tirelessly tore down
all the walls I had built
to mend
the broken bits
of my ugly heart
fixing what I had once believed
(because you start believing things
once they're said often enough)
that I'll always be
inadequate
but there
sans fear
or guilt
or shame
or doubt
you made me feel
worthy
when
you carved
your name
and
made me
yours: wife

Thank you
for not giving up
on me/ on us

for always fighting
fair and clean
with the fire
of lovers
who (still) make dreams
together
people in my past
fled
from my apartment
from my life
when things got hard
when they finally saw
beyond what's skin deep
but with you, I've learnt
we should always fight
fight hard
for the things that matter
the stuff that
truly matters
like the time
we stood for hours
on the cold cobblestones:
Dean Village
by the gurgling
Water of Leith
the breaking of an impasse
where we finally took
that terrifying
but bold
step

together
and forged
a future: family

Thank you
for being my rock
a safe space
solace
when the world gets
too much to bear
and the violence
of words
crashing waves
of self-doubt
seem to drown me
when my mind
broken, unhinged
splinters
swallowing me
into madness
as I lie on cold bathroom tiles
at 3am
tasting the salt of tears
upon my bitter tongue
wishing for amnesia
nobody else knows of
this perpetual darkness
that stains my soul
all the demons
I've fought/ am fighting/ still fighting

but with you by my side
I need no mask or labels
somehow with you
my armour withers and falls apart
crumbling into
stardust
(no more illusions)
the strident moment you
jump right in
diving headfirst
into the stormy depths of my soul
pull me into your embrace

Take my hand in yours
breathe my name in my ear
feed me medicine as I rest
my head upon your chest
following the hypnotic lull
of your beating heart
listening to the love song
it sings for me
master of the labyrinth of my mind
you are that difference
between heaven and hell
driving light into the darkest places
chaos calmed
anxiety and despair fades away
the voices in my head go still
and in your arms

I unfold, transform
into something all powerful
a mother goddess
of cosmic energy creating galaxies and stars
holding the universe and its blackholes inside me
potent
powerful
your tender kisses taste of sweet
promises: unconditional love
thank you, my dearest angel
(I don't say it enough)
(I don't say it enough)

Recipient of the National Arts Council's Arts Scholarship in 2018, NING CAI graduated from the University of Edinburgh with a Masters in Creative Writing (Distinction). Nominated for the Singapore Literature Prize, the bestselling author has seven titles under her belt and is now working on a series of children's books. Currently based in Switzerland with her spouse and their little boy, Ning can be contacted via her website NingThing.com.

A Letter in Seven Scenes

Marc Nair

Dear Carolyn,

I remember the beach at Batu Ferringhi in Penang, where we went for your childhood friend's wedding. I remember how you gelled your hair back and it was like you were a completely different person – striking, just as gorgeous.

I remember seeing two birds matching a pair of paragliders in the sky over the sea, swoop for swoop, thinking that it was a good omen for what was to come, along with a couple walking on the beach in the distance as the sun set behind the hills – another portent of love.

I remember being incredibly nervous after the wedding because I was going to surprise you with a wedding proposal at the swanky vegetarian restaurant I had researched for the occasion. But the restaurant was not where it should have been on the map. I sweated buckets as we wandered blindly down the road. You grew more irritated, even as the ring box pressed into my leg. Thankfully, the restaurant manifested not too far away. When we were done with dinner, I read you a poem (as I do), proffering a pair of elephant bangles before surprising you with the ring, a single blue sapphire. I got down on one knee while a wedding reception barrelled away in another part of the restaurant. And when you said yes, it was a feeling like nothing I have ever had before. Perhaps this is what joy should always feel like.

***

I remember the weekend of the last General Election. It was a week after you had gone for a knee operation. You were still on crutches. You had only left the house to visit the doctor but you did not want to miss your chance to vote. It was not easy; our stairwell is steep and it was a hot day, but you still made it to the community centre. The opposition party was new and its representatives felt young, untested, yet vibrant. Did they stand a chance? Not really. But they were standing up, even though they too walked with crutches. I was very proud of you as you hobbled towards the entrance, past the mural, determination in your eyes. Every vote counts, as they say, and you made yours count that day.

***

In Galle, our hotel was more of a homestay, a pattern we held to on that trip, the pace a languid stroll through city after city in the changeable south of Sri Lanka. But Galle was also the first taste of fresh air and Sri Lankan cooking, its distinctive spices and softer palate transporting us to a different world.

And that evening before dinner, we chanced upon locals basking on a windy evening, hoisting kites that lifted our spirits into the ether as families picnicked in grass not yet greened by the monsoon.

After Galle would come a bus ride to Mirissa, where you held yoga poses by the beach, where we ogled over doggies being walked and where we watched the rain fall from the shelter of a beachfront café. Where our room was haunted by an older man, but who left when we politely asked him to. Where we discovered the joy and terror of *kottu*, reconstituted prata.

The last homestay of our trip was in Kandy, in Ajit's house, where we were entranced by his dog, Mr Jack. Kandy was dry and dusty. We traced the footsteps of elephants during the Festival of the Tooth, but made sure we went back in the evening for Ajit's stories and his sumptuous cooking. That was yet another trip where animals seemed to be drawn to you – maybe because you hold space for them in your eyes. They bring you joy, just by being near you.

***

I remember our many years with the late Chubs Le Chat, a cat like no other. Your love opened the door for the cat to come in and find his home with us. He knew he was safe with you. He knew you had his back, no matter how many fights he got into, no matter how many quiet dawns he shattered with his yowling. He was an era of stories, and my love, you were right in the centre of his life, negotiating, crying, laughing with him. Even when his medical bills piled up, even when he was beginning the long decline from his fit, fighting days, you never flagged, never wavered. Even when his kidney began to decline and it got harder and harder to stick a needle into him to drip necessary fluids. Even when he disappeared for hours on end and returned, filthy, with matted blood and broken claws. And when we started The Chubs Mailbox and he got to know so many more lovely people in the neighbourhood.

If Chubs had written a poem to celebrate his life, this could be it:

Where I'm From

I am from
discarded boxes
and scratchy door rugs
fresh fish late at night
strangers quick to hug

From golden streetlights
and corridor runs
the belly of cars
in afternoon sun

I am from
shouting bouts with Bob
trespassing at times
random dogs being walked
all biscuits and grime

I'm from a home filled with
cuddles and kisses
a blanket that covers
and meets all my wishes

***

I remember Siargao, landing after messy connections from Cebu and walking right by a sign-up stand for the Siargao Marathon. I remember the clean roads, the wide spaces, the fresh air, the joy on your face. I remember getting on a motorcycle for the first time, and you holding onto me, and me hoping I would not crash, especially when we rode through a monsoon downpour, under the palm trees, down an empty road, gently undulating, with the wide sea opening at intervals beside us. I remember us in tiny villages, marvelling at the otherness of life, of reminiscing of the island we had lost back home, of the closeness to earth, to soil and the natural space. And I remember, back in the main town, how our hotel turned out to be a crapshoot of mosquitos, failed equipment and general discomfort and how you insisted we go to a better place, cough up the money for comfort and peace of mind. I was glad for that. It is not worth living as a backpacker past a certain point. I remember us riding around the island, plotting escapes to the beach in-between storms, finding the best pizza and *mahi* bowl on the island. Siargao was your little peace of mind, and I was glad to be there with you.

***

I remember Kazy-san's farm in the dead of winter, in the tiny hamlet of Kuta, north of Kyoto. It is not often you find a gem like this, and I was glad, because you became absolutely besotted with Kazy-san. I mean, who wouldn't be? The man could literally do anything: Grow rice, rear chickens, hunt deer (legally), make mochi, cook incredible meals. The house was cold, so we snuggled like hibernating beasts under the *kotatsu* and waited for the next meal to arrive. But we did put on our boots to walk the country roads and marvel at the emptied-out landscape, quiet, a picture of gentle decline. I think you are happiest at this intersection of nature and self, just having space to be, but quietly surrounded by competent people who know who they are and what they do. I want to always give that to you.

***

I remember our last trip together before the world shut down. We made it to Wonderfruit 2019 in Pattaya in December. We decided to spring for a tent with a fan near the festival grounds. Late at night, the bass notes rumbled under us like a nearby earthquake and the mornings were desert-hot. But we were in the heart of the festival, not ensconced in some distant hotel. There is a moment I remember, you walking down a slope, when I asked you to turn for a photo and the light catches you, glowing, perfect. I think that moment is imprinted on my mind forever, a resonant chord of joy, something that sums up the entirety of the festival: Lights, music, good food, art, meeting old friends, trying our hand at making different things, stretched out at night under stars, listening to the sounds of *molam* and leaping into a scooped-out lagoon to cool off in the morning.

***

Our stories with each other are far from done. Our memories are signposts to look back on, moments that are our well to draw meaning from, even as we find new ways to laugh, to argue, to cry, to be.

MARC NAIR is a poet who works at the intersection of art forms. He is currently pursuing projects that involve photography and creative non-fiction. His work revolves around the ironies and idiosyncrasies of everyday life. He has published 10 collections of poetry.

Which Came First – Love or Marriage?

Baskaran Narayanan

Dear Wifey,

It has been more than a decade since we met. It is time to look back: How did it all begin? Did we get married so that we can fall in love, or did we fall in love and then decide to get married?

At that time, we had both been very focused on our career and started looking for a soulmate only much later in life. A number of our peers were already either married or works-in-progress. So, we had to look outside our immediate social circle via dating services, friends and family. We were not just looking for a date, but a life partner.

The year-long run-up to our meeting was colourful, to say the least. I think I must have dated eight to nine ladies and you, at least a dozen guys.

We had each met one person we thought could be *the one*. But surprise, they did not like us back. Then we had ones we did not like, but they liked us and were unhappy we had felt otherwise. Then we had ones where both sides had to smile through the date because, well, the conversation was super boring. There was just no chemistry.

But we had to take our hats off to your guy accountant and my lady public relations person. On our respective first dates, we ended up arguing with them till our blood started to boil. Why on earth we would argue with people we had just met – on a date! – instead of just walking out, well, it beats me! But I guess we are people who will fight for principles and cannot just let things drop so easily.

Then came the intervention of our mothers. My Mom was having lunch at the staff canteen when a colleague told her she had a friend who knew someone whose daughter was looking for a husband.

So, my Mum got this friend's number and called her. The friend said: "Oh, not my daughter! She is still in primary school. But my daughter's tuition teacher, Ruby, has a friend who wants to settle down." And that someone was you.

Was this destiny? It seems like it when I think back on how we somehow made that connection to each other: My Mum < My Mum's colleague < My Mum's colleague's friend < My Mum's colleague's friend's tuition teacher < My Mum's colleague's friend's tuition teacher's friend = My wife!

Destiny? Or perhaps the famous Indian matchmaking network at work? Or both?

***

Time just flew by during our first date. I still remember it clearly: January 4 at Starbucks Novena. I think we must have talked for at least two hours. We were so comfortable with each other it felt like two old friends catching up after a long time.

A few more dates followed, then the meeting with your parents and mine. Before we knew it, the wedding registration was going ahead. Four months from the day we met, we were legally married. Within the year, we had our Hindu wedding. It seems amazing life events can happen so quickly when just a year ago, we were plodding from one date to another and wondering whether we should resign to being single.

Our honeymoon in New Zealand will always be one of my fondest memories. This was my first visit to New Zealand, the second for you. We touched down on a cold December evening; we walked out of the hotel looking for food at 7pm, but all the restaurants had already closed. Then, tucked away in an alley, we came upon a Thai eatery with just four tables. Small that shop might have been, but our hunger was anything but.

After a wonderful two weeks in New Zealand, back we came to the rest of our lives in Singapore.

***

But it was not easy in the beginning. We came from different backgrounds and we had different interests. We were married, but only just beginning to know each other.

Let's take something as simple as remembering a to-do list. You have such a fantastic memory! I, on the other hand, have good long-term memory but not so good in the short term. You can tell me something and within a few seconds, I would have forgotten it.

It took us five years to find a workaround! You started to WhatsApp me the to-do list instead of telling me verbally. On my part, I eventually got a fabulous to-do list app for my iPhone, complete with tags, folders, reminders, alerts and calendars. Better late than never, I guess.

***

And then parenthood came along.

It has been said that parenting opens up new avenues for various emotions: Joy, compassion, frustration, tenderness and most of all, sleep deprivation! Our two daughters have brought us closer, bonded us as a family, ensured we are never bored, never having too much money without knowing what to spend it on. They have brought amazing moments of joy and laughter to our life.

But it also means we barely have any time left for a quiet conversation together before some fight breaks out between them that needs our immediate attention. I miss our romantic Saturday dinners and the quiet Sunday mornings.

Thank goodness for Movie Date Night. While your parents help to watch over the kids, we sneak out of the house for a movie. And we continue to make time for each other so that at least once a month, we have our Saturday dinner out together. The kids are also older now, so the pieces have fallen well into place.

***

Now that we have been married for a decade, our work has had significant downturns for both of us. I left a stable public sector job to try my hand at business development. Crazy, yes, but it was an itch I had to scratch. But it was a disaster. I was no match for the tough corporate world. I could not hit my financial targets.

You were my rock during those times. You gave me the support to try something new and gave me the confidence I could turn things around, even if they did not work out. Eventually. I left the job and due to my good performance record, I was rehired by the public service. But those months between wanting to leave my corporate job and not getting a firm offer from the public service were agonising. But you were always there as my pillar of strength.

Then came your own plunge into the business world. You gave up your high-flying position to start your own business. I still remember the day you rang me frantically that a HDB site was up for tender and it was the location you had always wanted. Should you just bid for it? How much should you bid?

Going into business has always been your dream. I knew I had to stand by you, just as you had stood by me when I made my career switch. I knew in my heart you could do it, and it fills me with joy to see your business now breaking even and growing. If there is one accomplishment that I would highlight I am proud to have done for you, it is standing by you, no matter what anyone says about the pitfalls of starting a business during the pandemic. I am so happy to see you have proven the naysayers wrong.

***

So, which came first: Love or marriage? I realise love is not just an emotion. Yes, love is affection but it is also acceptance, like how you accept my dodo memory, or the sacrifices needed when we wanted to raise a family. Love is commitment: Standing by each other through the good and bad, the ups and downs. Never walking away from each other. Never giving up on each other.

Before we got married, we did not know each other very well. Unlike other couples who dated for years, we knew each other for just a few months. There was definitely affection but I would not compare that feeling to the affection we had built for, say, our parents, whom we have known all our lives. But now a decade later, that affection has grown by leaps and bounds, because we believe in each other and we want to make the relationship work.

I am truly grateful you have shared your life with me and I hope I have been a good husband to you. So, yes, love came first, not marriage. For without love, there is no life.

Yours lovingly,
Hubby

BASKARAN NARAYANAN works in the public sector. Outside of work, he spends time with his wife and two daughters playing games, watching movies and travelling.

Our Home on Quiet Avenue

Nuraliah Norasid

My dear partner, my best friend,

When I think of us right now, I find myself thinking about the home we have coming along, with tiles a lighter shade of cream where the contractor had hacked off bits of the floor and then re-tiled over. The flat this country expects us to live in, all of five years ago, when we barely knew what-was-what in the world; only that having a home, bearing children and living the middling, heteronormative life with an eye towards retirement and an ear plugged up with wool, is the standard and safest lifepath.

There is a strange chaos to transitory phases like this – between the collection of keys to the time we cross the threshold into a proper home, the floors wearing to shiny browning from numerous comings and goings, and the daily crossings from bedroom to kitchen to the living room, and back and back again.

Right now, wires hang, spilled like pulled entrails of some skinned animal. Entire sections of kitchen and dining area walls are screeded over with cement, the streaks and windshield-wiper arcs from hand trowels visible in the white and grey. Water, dirty with floating dust and dirt, pools in the bathroom, under pipes stuffed with cut bits of canvas sack, now that the fixtures and accessories have been removed. The newly-built kerbs for the shower screens look about as organic to the bathroom as a patch of pink grass in an abandoned soccer field, and we both wonder why the contractors did not build them flush against the line of the tiles.

Where we will live feels like a new suburbia. Flats in varying stages of renovation surround us and it is always so strange to me we never see many contractors at work, even though the units are already there. Just the traces of their work and their having-been-there: Fixtures yet-to-be-fixed, bags of cement and tiles left to the honour of thieves at drop-off points, the aftermath of handiwork in rough and dusty cement, the lone Good Morning tea towel on the floor.

Bicycle locks keep the gates shut, but leave the doors unlocked for us to swing open and peer into the living rooms of other flats, with their hacked-up floors and half-walls with broken edges; seeing what sort of air-conditioning units they have installed. Notes, calculations and floor plans are written on walls in marker and, looking at them in the silence of the new home, I am reminded of cave writings. Protected piping for aforementioned air-conditioning lay snake-coiled on ledges while we point to service yards from the comfort of our own.

We smell the salt of the sea where you used to work, and from the common areas of our soon-to-be block, you point at places where you used to berth. Was this shoreline different back then, before all these housing developments? Did the treeline undulate a line like a jagged mountain range from your view far out in the straits? I wonder, and I make a note to try and find out.

I have always found it fascinating the way these bits of life make meaning out of places I might have looked at but never did see. The cluster of steel lattice and industrial hues of Pelabuhan Johor Pasir Gudang and the wharves here on this island suddenly become peopled places. The ships sitting out in anchorage are less a picture of unmanned robot bodies going about some incomprehensible but nonetheless important work, and more a slow-moving theatre of memories I glimpse in a collage of jumpsuits, always-delayed text messages, the roulette game of trying to see if a call will make it through, and the short videos of bioluminescence in the waves sent from a faraway spot of blue on the world map.

Those memories seem so long ago, even when I was a part of it. Sometimes, these seven over years feel like 70, because of who we were and what we were doing – you sailing, studying for your class certifications; me trying to finish the edits to my thesis; us meeting for the first time at the now-gone McDonald's by Bras Basah Complex, meeting at our respective institutions for dinner and to try and study without distractions, and every argument that softened into the quiet discussions; and silences heart-breaking, dreadful and realising as moments of mourning

– they seem so far away, belonging to people we are no longer.

The conferment of my doctorate feels like a lifetime ago (and the young woman who received it a slim, slightly less tired version of me). We have both gone through several jobs, gained several more inches in our girths and have knees and backs that hurt when we sit down or try to get up. Grocery runs and perusing kitchen hoods and air-conditioning units are date highlights. And we are collectively frustrated by Boomer logic and puzzled by Gen Z humour, sandwiched as we increasingly are – financially, generationally, and ideologically it seems – between the two. Most days are quietly spent at home, playing Bloons TD6 like filthy casuals on our phones. I wonder if we have grown just that much older at the end of every YouTube video we watch to fall asleep.

***

Here is the thing about homes and lives; almost everyone is going to have opinions about them. That our home is going on the second floor has already drawn every negative comment, every concern from almost everybody we know. The way people talk, one would imagine the second floor of every HDB block to be some of kind of slum, harbouring all kinds of illegal activities and lowlifes. It is an issue I had not thought and cared about before. But after hearing numerous "Why didn't you get a higher floor?", every concern of whether the smell from the waste collection centre would rise and settle like miasma on our floor, whether stray animals would wander up and drag garbage with them; seeing the shift from neutrality to subtle grimace of pity in the countenance of their faces, I find myself inundated with a sense of inadequacy and inferiority.

I hear it, where you may not: the undertones of what the second floor is often associated with. Not a home, not value, not comfort or cleanliness, not good financial status, not race or class privilege. If it is just me, I would have taken these comments as air because what has been said to me about my race and class (and religion) that I have not heard before? If it is just me, I would sit alone with the sense of being less, feeling like a criminal in every shop that I walk into, feeling like I have to constantly justify myself to every shopkeeper for buying just "one small thing", and feeling a sense of panic that for some inexplicable reason, my card would not work when I try to use it.

But it is not just me and because it is not, my race and the class I grew up in often feel encumbering when they never should be. I feel like a weak link in an awful chain ladder up to some inconsequential social standing I never wanted to reach. Not for lack of drive or ambition, no, but for the fact that gaining any kind of standing with anyone and in any society has never been my life's interest or goal.

Because it is not just me, fear has taken on a new and monstrous set of anxieties: Will this shade of green on our walls be "too Malay"? Will this jewel tone for our curtains be "too Hari Raya"? Will this hue of lighting look "too cheap"? It seems the beauty standard for homes of "good standing" among homeowners our age are white walls, neutral tones, and minimalist simplicity. That our home will be on the second floor, I feel, leads us to we have this intrinsic need to overcompensate.

For whom, exactly?

Call me an idealist, but when it is just us, that house is not a second-floor flat with a conflicted sense of identity and the weight of (dis)regard – all 24 storeys of it – upon its shoulder. It is not a space with money-making potential when at some point, someone is going to deem it ready to be flipped around for some shoebox apartment in a condominium.

I see the morning sun coming in beams through the living room window, that we would open on a Saturday morning for a bit of air. I sure hope I will have my sleep schedule sorted out so that I might enjoy more mornings than I do evenings.

You might think we would be worrying about children screaming from the playground below but with tuition, extra-extra-curricular, and smartphones, how many children play anymore?

The laundry would be drying on the rack in the service yard. We might have to do it in batches when it is time to change the sheets. Somewhere in a pool of morning light, our cat might be languishing, though it is more likely she is hiding somewhere for a quiet, uninterrupted nap because you know how handsy I get with her. There might be something boiling in a pot on the kitchen hob you have spent so much time and research to buy. What is boiling is likely the sweet potato I have to keep reminding myself to cook before they start to root. I would be opening the door of the refrigerator at least 10 times a day. Not to take anything out from it, just to take a look and feel calm at the fact it is stocked, and no one is going to go hungry in our home.

The bookshelves stretch floor to ceiling. You remind me to keep it neat. I will find whatever nook and cranny I can to slip in a book, stacking it over those shelved upright. There will be little trinkets here and there we will try to keep dust-free for a time before boxing them all up and stashing away in a box somewhere. You will keep joking about formaldehyde poisoning from the books, but we both know we should worry less about that and more about whether I will fall off the bookshelf ladder when my ankles are no longer as steady as they used to be.

The robot vacuum will be the life in a quiet house, as the cat has darted off to hide from it. I imagine it to be a little Wall-E, alone amongst the vestiges of the once-living. If some catastrophe befalls Earth one day, would our smart homes and gadgets carry on with their routines? The alarms and actions that have been pre-set, playing songs and tunes at ever increasing volumes, switching on air-conditioners and living room lights in preparation for the evening? At what point in the time after humanity would the last of our power die away?

These are the questions we entertain each other with in that time between wakefulness and sleep. When to say things, ask things we need no answer to, like the day you asked, eyes going from sleep-heavy to alert, "How Singapore reconciled its relationship with Japan in the years following the Japanese Occupation? How long did that take? How did it happen?".

Some things, as I have learnt, may not always come with a reconciliation. Perhaps this one does, as you spent the next half hour reading articles about it on your phone. Some nights I lay in bed, unable to sleep because I think of the bridges I might just have to burn in order to continue having these moments with you. What would I do when there comes a time I can no longer be in my family's life? I think of my mother who does her best to be accepting in her own indirect way, the life she has led and how I cannot be another thing she has lost after health and her own family. I think of my youngest brother who is always forgotten and overlooked for how quietly he manages his own matters.

And then I think, the only reason I can have this life now, with the headspace and resources to help my family, is because I know I can wholly trust and take comfort in what I am going home to; the quiet moments, somewhere where I know I can sequester myself away to write and read and freak out over a million deadlines if I need to, and all the worries and frustrations I have, have some place to be aired without fear of judgment or censure.

So, when I think of us right now, I think of the tranquil air as it floats with the sunbeams into the corner we have designated as my study (because we both know how the sounds of other people working and typing, breathing and chewing grate on my nerves when I am trying to focus). I hear the muffled sounds from your gaming and YouTube car videos coming from the closed doors of your designated 'cave', just a few paces from the kitchen. The time is in the afternoon, that really lazy time between lunch and dinner. You might take a nap at some point. You will be thinking of cleaning the bathrooms or that it is time to look over the markets. I will be trying to work quietly, worrying about a dozen things all at once. But I know, night would come to this house, as it would to all beings, and we would have our phones, our co-op games, and questions to which we need no answers.

Yours,
Nuraliah

NURALIAH NORASID is a writer and educator. She is the author of *The Gatekeeper*, which won the Epigram Books Fiction Prize (EBFP) in 2016, as well as several short stories and essays published in journals, magazines and anthologies, including *Singa-Pura-Pura: Malay Speculative Fiction from Singapore*, *A View of Stars: Stories of Love*, *Budi Kritik*, *The Epigram Collection of Best New Singaporean Short Stories, Volume Three*, *Mynah Magazine*, and *Perempuan: Muslim Women Speak Out*. Outside of caregiving, teaching and writing, Nuraliah enjoys video gaming and walking.

Creating Our Love Map and
Coming Full Circle

Anisa Hassan

Dearest Hazik,

I cannot remember when was the last time I wrote to you, although I know I must have written hundreds in the last three decades we have been together.

However, this is the letter that has taken me the longest, as I am equally nervous and excited to pen my thoughts and feelings. Our children would probably roll their eyes when they read this: Why is Mum embarrassing us with TMI (too much information)? Our friends would probably see a side of us they have never seen before. Most concerning for me is how readers would perceive and judge the real love story of a matchmaker?

How much is too much and what is best left unsaid?

I got really lucky in this lifetime because I met you when I was 17. We met at a time when we both had no money, no status and no clue how our friendship was going to pan out. I was a bumbling, bright-eyed girl who was working hard to lift myself from a life of mediocrity and there you were, a picture of cool confidence and calm composure. Little did I know then you had a slight stammer and that was why you hardly spoke! I must admit, that stammer soon disappeared because, what can I say, I brought out the poet in you! But damn, those sharp features and deep-set eyes!

Now as a matchmaker and seeing firsthand how so many clients suffer needlessly from their fears, doubts and what a relationship should look like, I cannot be more grateful our paths had crossed when ignorance was still bliss and 'twas a folly to be "wise".

I remember how I used to look forward to our daily bus rides after school. We took bus number 25 from Bedok Interchange to Ang Mo Kio Interchange, and then another bus to Hougang. Like a gentleman, you always made sure I got home safely. What a complete waste of time (on hindsight) but oh, how those precious times sealed our friendship!

Now that I have more than 30 years of data to crunch, allow me to count the ways why I love you more today than I ever did before. One thing that stood out, across space and time: The undeniable fact you were always there for me.

You were there in my "fumbling" teenage years when I wanted to break free from my father's overwhelming control and my mother's dependence on me to deal with her family feud at that time. I was resentful I had to step up and be her voice. You were there to listen patiently to my endless woes and entertain my whims for hot *cheng tng* at a moment's notice.

You were there in my "fitting-in" 20s when I was made to feel insignificant by the Bosses who tried to silence me as a journalist. There was tacit bullying by Superiors who condemned me for having an opinion and questioning their authority. It was an uncomfortable and challenging period for our relationship too, as you were away in the US and had to listen to my long-drawn tirade over a weekly 20-minute, $10-phone-card-long-distance call – our routine for close to four years! I remember writing down important points I wanted to share with you because our Friday night chats were very sacred and special.

When June 1998 rolled along, I was never more sure-footed about being with someone for the rest of my life. I remember shedding so much tears on our wedding day, not just because I am now married to my best friend, but because I finally found complete freedom being with you. Never have I felt tied down because you knew how to set me free. Even in those early years, your trust in me was so strong there was never a need to control.

You were there in my "fiery, focused" 30s as we built our family together. You were instrumental in giving me the courage, confidence and capital to start our dating business, which set our lives on a different trajectory from then on. Your foresight convinced me that matchmaking is not that different from journalism, because the dating industry also demands high-value people skills, genuine curiosity and a talent for tuning in to people's problems. You knew me more than I knew myself and with every step I took as an entrepreneur, the belief became more entrenched I could soar as high as I imagined and achieved anything I wanted, because you would always have my back.

I witnessed how you resented unfairness and took control of the situation when I started raising funds from possible investors. As much as it was frustrating when many potential investments fell through because you could see it was a one-sided deal, I did not quite know how to appreciate your brash and abrasive ways at that time. Do not get me wrong – your abrasiveness is still there! But at least now, I know why and I actually find it endearing, if painfully so.

Now we are both well into the deep-end of our 40s. I must say this is the period I cherish the most as we grow and age as a couple. Starting from the unexpected call from Muis (Islamic Religious Council) inviting us to perform our Hajj in 2013, our journey so far has gone through numerous peaks and valleys. Everything else before just seemed like a walk in the park.

I thought it was time for me to return the favour and let you further your studies and pursue your passion in finding an alternative solution to a fairer, ethical and more inclusive financial system. I thought I would have your back this time. Promising to take care of the kids, our home and our business while you became a student again, I felt a deep sense of responsibility that I must follow through. Knowing how exhausted you must feel, having to shuttle between two cities in a week, I shielded you from a myriad of problems I was dealing with, both at home and work.

I was focusing our communication more on you, your adjustment to your student life as a PhD candidate, your new friends, your mentor and your general well-being. On hindsight, I was trying to compensate for the time when you had put me front and centre in your life and graciously allowed me to bask in the limelight of my professional success.

I did not want you to spend a moment worrying about me, the children, my parents or our business and that was my greatest folly. I had put on a brave front for far too long and when the time compelled me to start living more authentically, I was put on an unstoppable losing streak. There was no way I could stop things from falling apart; I could no longer grasp the reality that felt like a string of pearls coming undone.

It started with me losing *Abah* in August 2016 and I had to immediately shoulder the responsibility of caring for *Mak* and not wanting to lose her next. But focusing more attention on family meant diverting attention away from our business. It was not long before the business unravelled with the license to operate coming to an abrupt end. I felt like I was being punished for not being truthful to you; I felt like I had let you down because our sustenance was being constricted. Without a business, I put our family on the brink of financial collapse. Quietly, I struggled to do all I could to keep going because coming clean meant having to admit I was wrong.

This is the first time I am putting it out there that I was wrong. I was wrong to shield you from all my troubles; I was wrong to second guess your reaction if I had told you the truth; I was wrong to assume I had it all figured out, when all the signs were telling me to stop sliding further down the rabbit hole.

For all the anguish, frustration and sadness I have put you through, I am deeply sorry.

This was the reset button both of us needed to re-evaluate what is important in our lives.

Of all the losses I had had to endure and all the possessions I had to forgo, the one thing I would fight to the edge of the world to win, is our marriage. During that vulnerable time when we could have broken apart, our relationship, by God's grace, got solidified. This defining moment made me realise I am not where I am because of my own effort, my fame or my cleverness. Instead, this period clearly revealed how you have always been my pillar of strength. You taught me to stay true and humble, even when I am in the limelight. And if I can see further in the distance, it is only because you have allowed me to stand on your shoulders.

You helped me get centred again and encouraged me to stay true to my mission, which has always been grander than the two of us put together. I have continued to stay the course and dug deeper than before because you have always believed I am slated for bigger and better things. That conviction was enough to pull me through one of the darkest periods of my life and it was not long before we reinvented our business to become what it is today.

And there is nothing like a pandemic to make me realise what is essential in life. We have found ourselves in uncommonly challenging times and as we look down the barrel of lockdowns and stricter business protocols, not knowing how we will survive this wild ride. But my heart is at peace, knowing I can lean on you.

For the first time in as long as I can remember, we get to spend every waking hour together. In fact, there had never been a time when we are in each other's company 24/7. As I sit from across your desk in the office, I am filled with an abiding sense of gratitude for the love and deep connection we still have, even after all these years.

For one, I love that I am not going through this period all by myself and (almost) every day you make me feel seen, heard and valued. Without missing a beat, I know you are always working behind the scenes to propel me forward every time my story gets published in the media. I know you are proud of me, as much as I am proud of the three books you have written and published. I promise to at least read one of them before my 50th birthday!

I love that you do not try to change me and give me the assurance I can always have a different view from you. Happily-ever-after is a bit overrated because no two persons from different backgrounds and experiences can ever come together and have zero arguments or clash of opinions.

And since having hard conversations is unavoidable, we may as well get good at it. Even then, before a discussion gets too heated, we have learnt to drop it and respect our differences and honour our peace. I know it is hard for you sometimes to initiate a conversation after an argument because you needed the acknowledgement you were right. This is where I am adept at reeling you back to what truly matters. The more prolonged the silence, the more impatient I get at how much time has been wasted in sulking. There are always a million and one things to talk about – the kids, the cat, the family, the friends, the business, the clients and the latest cycling milestone on Strava.

I also love that instead of road trips, we indulge in long drives and – during this pandemic – this would be driving from home to Changi Airport and then to Jurong West to pick up a pre-loved chair you bought on Carousell! I especially love that we get to reclaim our carefree days as teens again. I appreciate how, like other Singaporeans, we had made that spontaneous beeline for a quick ice cream in the heart of Woodlands, the night before the phase two (heightened alert) kicked in. I love that we share many common friends who, even when we cannot meet in large groups, could still share durians with us by the Yishun dam.

My connection with you lies in our everyday choices of looking out for each other rather than grandiose gestures. I notice how much I look forward to you placing the *teh si* gently on my desk every morning when I start my day at work. I appreciate how much you rush to get me a Burger King whopper meal whenever I have 30 minutes in-between meeting clients. It reminded me so much of our days as poor students.

As we are about to enter the next big decade, I want you to know I no longer need very much to stay happy with you. Sure, a trip to catch the Aurora Borealis in Iceland would be fun someday. For now, know that I deeply and completely cherish our small moments – doing our grocery runs when you make sure I carry only the lightest plastic bag; parking illegally and gleefully by the side of the road just to buy Shadoe's pet food; and late-night *pratas* to satisfy your cravings even after I have brushed my teeth and would rather be sleeping at 10pm. I know love is a verb and from your actions, I know I am loved.

I am grateful even though our children are now charting their own paths, our experience together continues to get better and more exciting. When we started our journey, what we had was just a blank map. And as we made mistakes

and learned from them, we filled out more of that map. No matter how much I secretly wish I already know everything about you, there is always more of the map to fill out. Still, no matter where our journey will take us, with you, I am always home.

I am forever yours, faithfully… (cue Journey)
Anisa

ANISA HASSAN learned about relationships from a very early age, being the 9th child in a family of 10. She understands the concept of getting along with her parents and siblings to further the fulfillment of her needs. She has a high level of tolerance for diverse views and beliefs, being one of the few Muslim girls in a Methodist school. Little did she know her formative years would positively impact her love for people from all backgrounds in her professional life. Now a business owner of an online and offline matchmaking agency, Anisa has spent the last 20 years protecting her clients' right to be loved and helping thousands of her local and international clients walk down the aisle.

Co-conspirators in Life's Jig

Tara Dhar Hasnain

My Darling,

As I sit down to write to you from my heart, I am tongue-tied, a bit like the day you proposed to me years ago.

Memories of that epoch come crowding my mind and I am transported to a time of such excitement, of immense joy, when waking up each morning my heart was filled with anticipation of what the day might bring.

It all started slowly and quietly, a friendship forged through joint homework as graduate students, especially reading poetry together. Oh, the fun of studying Yeats and TS Eliot and "prepping" for the MA examination with each other! Though a keen student, I had never imagined that cooperative study could be so much fun!

What an exciting and stimulating time it was! We were part of a larger group of friends, going out together for coffee, hanging out between classes, mulling over English literature, discussing exciting texts. Till, one day, when our group met again after the long two-month summer break, you suddenly turned just to me, and very softly said something like "I missed you terribly". At that point, I realised how deep was our mutual friendship, how much I, too, had missed being with you – our recognition of a mutual bond that had almost sneaked up on me. Just having a cup of coffee with you was unlike anything I had felt before!

Later that year, you proposed marriage. At first, I was left speechless. I had just not thought about our relationship that way, us being from very different backgrounds; me born into a Hindu Brahmin household, you into a Muslim family. I was scared to risk converting my relationship with you, my best friend, into marriage. What if it did not work out as a couple? I would lose my best friend as well, a double loss. And yet, as you reminded me, such a friendship was exactly the best basis for a wonderful long-term relationship.

A few years later, once we were both working, we took the plunge, in spite of some naysayers and prophets of doom who forecast our marriage would dissolve within a year! It is now 50 years since you proposed to me, and 47 since we married each other. And I would not exchange our life together, even with its ups and downs, for anything else. Our days together, practically all of our adult life, pass like a movie before me, and once again I am back in that early time, with that early self, feeling that sense of joy and excitement!

You were such a rock in the stormy moments when I faced some pressure to break off with you – helping me to stay the course, refusing to give up on our new-found happiness! Thank you, my dearest, for the unflinching faith that we could work it all out.

We had a few lovely months together as a couple, but then came a big change. I won the Commonwealth scholarship to Oxford University to do research – a dream project. But it meant a long separation of two years or more from you, in those days before cheap or affordable flights. Once again, you stood by me, insisting I should grab this wonderful, once-in-a-lifetime opportunity, so I left for England, though with a heavy heart.

The next few years were a bit tough, though we did manage to meet for short breaks at my parents' house in Vienna, me flying there from Oxford, you from India. Later, when the Indian Government granted you study leave for an MBA, you joined me at Oxford University. From then on, life just got better and better. We enjoyed being together, always bound to each other by invisible knots of love, and a deep mutual regard for and understanding of each other.

A defining moment in our lives came when you resigned from your cushy civil service job to take the risk of working for an American multinational. Yet we were confident it would be fine, as long as it made you happy about your work – which it did – over your long career.

We took all such major life decisions together, discussing the pros and cons, going for what would make us happy, even if it seemed a less prestigious option.

After some years, we decided to start a family, and our son, Aftab, was born in Geneva. I think back to our happy years there as a small family - our weekend forays into the rest of Switzerland, or driving to nearby French towns like Evian or Henniez for a meal, drinking Evian water from the spring itself. Do you remember the scramble to get to

Chamonix, to take the *telepherique* (gondola) to the top of Mont Blanc, the highest Alp, in time for the mist to clear? Those were the days!

Many weekends we spent in the Swiss village of Gruyeres, going into the castle with our little son, who loved to walk along the ramparts and imagine fighting off invading armies, followed by fondues or raclettes served with their own fresh cheese! The snow brought winter fun on skis, under cold yet bright skies. It was a great way to get warmed up, to be in the strong and bright Alpine sun, and to troop back home in the evening, tired yet happy.

So it went for some years. We continued to enjoy each other's love and companionship. Life kept us busy as two young adults, managing careers along with bringing up a small child, but we shared the fun as well as the tough days, and hardly ever felt hassled or overburdened. We enjoyed living in beautiful Switzerland, going up to the mountains, or to well-known wine-growing areas to sample the fresh crop of wines. And each year, we made the trek to nearby Montreux for its Jazz Festival, introducing our young son to the music we enjoyed. Evenings were for bedtime stories, putting the little one to bed, followed by some quiet time together, just you and me.

When our son was seven, our moves to Asia as expats started. We enjoyed those experiences as well, treating them as exciting opportunities to live in different countries and learn about new cultures. We went to Bali over the first school break in Jakarta, and later, also to other countries in the region.

We lived in Indonesia, then in Singapore, and thence to India for some years. That was great too, going back to live in our own country after nearly two decades of being away, almost our whole adult lives up to that point. It was also wonderful for Aftab to have more time with his grandparents, and learn proper Hindi, India's national language.

I went back to teaching at Delhi University, a position I had resigned from years ago, when we left India. You felt very happy to see me doing work I thoroughly enjoyed, being with young people on the cusp of adulthood. As always, you had encouraged me to apply to teach there once again, knowing it would mean a lot to me. You seemed to feel my pulse better than I did myself, many a time!

Next, we moved to the US, a very exciting country to live in, and that was another adventure.

But after some years came an upheaval no one could really ever be ready for. One very cold January day, as Minneapolis lay covered in snow, out of the blue, our son, now a young man of 20, died in the middle of the night. For a while, we were shattered, we could not make sense of life anymore; it seemed so much against the course of nature. The words spoken by Shakespeare's Macbeth soon after the death of his wife:

I have lived long enough: my way of life
Is fallen into the sere, the yellow leaf

now took on a new meaning. What use was it for us to continue to live when the light of our lives was gone? What a dark time it was! We could not see a clear pathway out of this abyss. We felt bereft, marooned, far from our parents and many old friends in India, far away in the Midwest of America, in the middle of a cold, bleak winter. But we rode it out together; our love and support for each other helped us through those nightmarish days and nights.

On the very first morning after our son had passed away, do you recall as I was making some tea in our bright, spacious kitchen cum family room, I said to you that Afab must have broken free of all bonds, free as a bird now, and we suddenly saw a bright red cardinal fly down and sit on the deck outside for minutes on end, his red body etched clearly against the thick carpet of white snow? As a small child, Aftab, for every birthday, or Mother's or Father's Day, had made cards for us, and signed his name along with a big red heart, to say "I love you". Was this him again, showing us he was now free, but that he loved us still?

With one voice, we both decided on a multi-faith service to honour our child, who had been brought up as a good, ethical, caring human being. After the over-full service, we heard back from hundreds of friends, who said they had never attended such a deeply moving, multi-faith service, a fitting memorial to our secular-minded son.

Our many friends rallied round us from day one and gave us deeply-valued physical and emotional sustenance. Since we did not practise any faith, they took turns to stay home with us, and brought over more food than we could consume. They sat with us, listened to us, holding us in their circle of love and care. Family members, too, those who could fly over, came over, to help us slowly find our feet. We were like little children learning to walk again, in a new and changed world.

And it really was a new world for us. As we started meeting people again, if anyone just asked me a common and innocent question like, "Do you have children?", it was enough to make me tear up, not knowing how to respond. Should I say "No, I don't" (that seemed to belie Aftab's whole existence)? Or "I did, but I don't any more"? Life's simplest situations were like traps laid for us. Yet we kept trying, and our friends kept getting us to join in the rhythm of normal life again. If I broke down and cried, you would hold me tight, and reassure me till the intensity of grief abated a bit. And I did the same for you.

Friends told us the statistics were stacked against parents who had lost a child, with 85 per cent of them divorcing. But this seemingly unending night actually worked the other way for us. Over time, it brought us closer than I would have thought possible. If I felt down, you would hold me up, reminding me of the happy times, and assure me you were there for me, forever and through everything. And I did the same for you. We became fonder of each other, realising the preciousness of our closeness, in the face of the fragility of life.

As time passed, the wound became less raw, and we slowly learnt to laugh again, to participate in life's round of joy and sorrow. We decided that since we had been left on earth after Aftab was gone, we must live our lives with some grace and try to bring happiness to other young people.

After some thought, we established scholarships at various educational institutions and among various under-served communities, to enable young people to pursue a college education, something Aftab had really cared about, as well as making donations to TRP, or Theater in the Round, a very old community theatre in Minnesota, because Aftab used to love to act in plays.

We also turned our attention to our ageing parents, who could not recover fully from the shock of losing their first grandchild, and for my parents, their only grandchild. Minneapolis now seemed even further away from India than before.

After a year or two, your company moved us, a sort of temporary, "soft" move, to Singapore, a place we had enjoyed living in two decades earlier. For a few years, we kept shuttling between Singapore and Minneapolis, interspersed with frequent visits to India. Then, in 2008, you were transferred back to Minneapolis. At that point, you asked for early retirement, and we opted to make our home in Singapore, which was just a short direct flight to Delhi.

Here, we settled down with some of our old friends from 1990, plus made many new ones. You encouraged me to go back to work again, and I taught for some years at the Singapore Management University. Then, an editing opportunity fell into my plate, and I took it. I have really enjoyed this new line of work; it was very close to university teaching in many ways. You helped me find my feet and, as before, showed great faith in me. If I expressed any doubts about this new, though allied, career path, you shared your belief I would enjoy it, and you were spot on. I enjoy the work itself, as well as the friendships with a number of authors based in Singapore.

Something very significant for my inner growth also crystallised in Singapore and in this, too, you played a significant and meaningful role. Over the years, I had become increasingly keen to bring Buddhist principles into my daily life. My father had already introduced me to the Buddha long ago, as a child. When living in the US, I used to fly to New York to attend teachings by His Holiness the Dalai Lama almost every year. Yet I remained somewhat sceptical and questioning, suspicious of any "religious" path. But once we moved to Singapore, I began to miss my regular connection with a Buddhist community and with Buddhist teachings. Here, it was hard to find any such teachings in English, as most were in Mandarin.

Sensing my frustration, you went on the Internet, to find a good fit for me. Within hours, you told me about ABC, the Amitabha Buddhist Centre, a Tibetan-Buddhist style local chapter of an international Buddhist organisation, the FPMT.

They offered regular teachings on texts by famous Buddhist masters. All were either in English or translated into English. You would come home from work and drive me to

this centre in Geylang and also pick me up afterward. In the initial weeks, when I still felt hesitant, you encouraged me to try it out. Quite soon, I settled in, and this proved a godsend, providing a wonderful spiritual centre for my life.

Thank you, my dearest, for doing all this. It means the world to me.

There is so much more to talk about, like what you said about my hands once – it made me look at myself with new eyes! Or the way you supported my growing interest in museums, history, heritage and allied subjects. As always, you have been my backbone, supporting me with your unconditional love, expressing your faith that I can do anything I put my mind to. Just like my father once did when I was a girl.

I am extremely fortunate to have your deep love, and your belief in me. No one could have asked for more in the adventure of life. Ever since I found your love, I have never felt alone or abandoned. In hard times, it has given me courage and in good times, we have found a level of happiness not to be found easily. I have the "double happiness" of my best friend being my life partner too! If I have reciprocated even a fraction of that, I will rest content.

With all the love and affection I bear you, my first and only love,

Yours always,
Tara

TARA DHAR HASNAIN has been a university teacher for the major part of her life, including at Singapore Management University and LASALLE College of the Arts in Singapore. A decade ago, she moved into editing and continues to work as a freelance editor. She is also active in heritage and museum-related activities. Tara has given talks at the museums and published articles on these topics, including on Kashmir's syncretic heritage. She enjoys reading, music, learning about new cultures and lots else!

Dear You. Here goes...

Laila Jaey

I think we all have cracks – big ones, little ones. Rich people, poor people – we all have them. And these cracks happen from the stories we have been told and the stories we tell ourselves. Or they arise from our perceptions, shaped by our voices and the voices of others.

Growing old means we now have the distance to take a good, hard look at how and why these cracks are there in the first place. As my 50th year looms, I wonder, as I wander over my cracks: How many of these are skewed by multiple narratives told over the years? How many of these should I say are mine, how many from the hurts inflicted by others? Can I seek restitution if they were not entirely my fault? Or do I have the choice to forget?

There is some peace in forgetting. And I have been so good at forgetting I think it has festered into an actual condition. Except some things refuse to fade away. They may have metamorphosised each time I retold them differently in my head, through the different stages of my life.

Do you know many of my cracks have to do with you? Many of them have also healed because of you. I know you have your own cracks too, though you may not have thought about them the way I do. Maybe because you do not want to acknowledge them.

This enrages me. How can someone not want to reflect? Are you scared? Is it because you do not know there is a way to look at it without feeling like a failure? Or are you incapable of awareness?

After all these years, I do not think you really know who I am. I know you think I am capable and difficult, that I have been unfair to you because you have done the best you can. Still, it is not enough.

I have told you many times about how I feel. I have ranted about it. I have tried to show you my hurt. But your military training has kept you stoic and silent. You have been trained not to respond. Are you with me because you want that medal of fortitude? The one that says you do not quit in the face of bullets and bombs? Are you loyal because it is a creed?

But your inability – or perhaps paralysis – to engage in my chronic paranoia has worn me down. You do not see how you trigger me when you do not respond to my verbal and physical throw-ups, when I need someone to set me straight. You let me become irrational and abusive. Maybe you believe I do so because you have not been able to give me my self-worth. When you gave me my ring, you said this is good enough.

I had accepted your ring because I wanted stability. Perhaps I knew then there would not be anyone else. And perhaps I also understood you could be right about my self-worth. But I showed you, didn't I? In all our years together, haven't I shown you I can be responsible, level-headed and do whatever is necessary so we do not fall backwards?

What I want is a partner, a healer, a rationale man who can plan, think ahead, and evolve with me. But you do not seem to feel there is a need to, despite me telling you about the tornado inside me. You are not my pillar of strength, though you are a pillar nonetheless, a structure for me to cling to.

Still, I am on shaky ground. Sometimes, I think you are still here because you do not want our only child to be a statistic. You do not want our daughter to be from a broken home. Neither do I. But she is a smart young lady with my intuition and your silence. She can see what we are going through and she articulates it in her eyes. Mum, stop it, she says. Dad, you need to do better. I look back and tell her: But this is who we are.

I know you have probably thought of leaving – and if we had not had a kid, you would probably have left a long time ago. Your commitment is to the family more than it is to me and I cannot fault you for that. But I can learn to honour your commitment. I also need to find a way to reframe this situation without offending my truth.

I still love you. For reasons I never expected love to be. But I am conflicted if you are determined to commit. And whether you will do what it takes to keep us together. Yes, I am hard to understand. Yes, I do not hide my criticisms. I am a committed, maniacal, over-worked teacher while you are the under-achiever with a pot of untapped potential which you are not interested to unearth.

So, let me tell you: I am not going anywhere. I do not want to seek mental help – it is becoming such a cliché. We have created this jazz music together because we have each played different notes. It is chaotic. And sometimes, it ends abruptly – I am aware of that. But I do not want to lie and say things will get better if we work at it.

This letter is an outpouring, a recognition of my fears and my failures. And yes, of my love. Even though it is becoming quite hard to think about the good times – honestly, we have not nearly put in enough effort to create it – and even though I know there is always the possibility I may be happier if you were not around, I do not want it.

Perhaps love is about acknowledging we can be both right and terribly wrong. Thomas Hardy (you know I cannot end this letter without going back to this great English writer) said that people go on marrying because they cannot resist natural forces, although many of them know perfectly well they are "possibly buying a month's pleasure with a life's discomfort". Well, to be honest, we did not even have a month's pleasure (remember the honeymoon with the family?).

But I will take this life of discomfort. If not for anything else, it means we are honest and committed. What a crackpot of a thing to say, huh?

LAILA JAEY is a Singaporean mother of one who has been in the media industry for over 20 years. She enjoys working from home and hopes to continue writing about her long-suffering spouse.

We Will Always Find Our Way Back to Each Other

Shirlene Noordin

Dear Raphaël,

It is our 10th wedding anniversary today as I write this letter to you and it feels a little awkward. Our digital lives have made letter writing such a lost art I am having trouble thinking in long form.

This act of writing down my feelings makes me feel a little vulnerable. Being a little self-conscious, I have always shied away from bold declarations of love and affection. This could explain why I have never written a love letter to you before, nor indulged in big celebratory gestures like giving gifts and springing surprises on anniversaries or birthdays. I know you understand, because you are like me.

So, where do I start? What do I want to say in a letter I have not already said in person? Maybe I can begin by telling you how I am so happy to be married to you. We have been together for 17 years. That is a long time! We did not think marriage was necessary, since we were already doing so well together as a couple. But now that we are, I am so glad we had made that commitment. How amazing it is we have journeyed this far. I am so grateful for what we are and what we share. Have I even told you this before? Even if I have, it is probably not enough.

But since we are 10,000km apart, this letter can perhaps be a poignant way to mark this milestone year. As before, we are again separated by distance, a reality of our cross-cultural, transnational relationship. We knew it was never going to be easy. There were once obvious obstacles that stood in our way – the physical distance and cultural differences. How many times have we experienced long separations because you had to be in France for work or to be with your family? Just like right now.

With the Covid-19 pandemic still hovering over us, being apart has only heightened the sense of separation. You always tell me we will always find our way back to each other, no matter how long the separation, and that is so true. But no matter how often this happens, it is never easy to say goodbye when either one of us has to leave. To this day, my heart is heavy whenever I see you off at Changi Airport and it still does somersaults when I greet you there upon your return.

We have never had a problem with being from different cultures. We have embraced them both and internalised them. In fact, this is what makes our relationship so interesting. I love that we are curious about and respect each other's culture. I love that we are always able to learn something new about our cultural histories, cuisines and languages.

Despite these differences, we have managed to bridge the gap. And because of these differences, we have never taken each other for granted. But we have also found so much in common. From our two cultures, our two worlds, we have forged something that is now uniquely ours. I want to tell you how special this is. It is a world where I find comfort and understanding, where I feel most at home and where I am completely myself. This world of ours makes me feel safe and loved.

We have always made decisions together as a couple and this is something I really value. I like the democracy of our marriage. We are always on an equal footing. I like that you take this equality so seriously. You make sure to consult me on everything – from household matters, making plans with friends, right down to the bigger issues. How mad you would get at me whenever I make plans with friends for both of us without discussing them with you first because, as you say, you would never do that to me!

At first, I did not quite understand why you would make such a big deal of something so small, especially when I knew you had nothing else on your schedule. And when we have to do home repairs or renovations, you always tell the contractors you have to consult with your wife first. They probably think you are under my thumb!

But I slowly began to understand why. It is always important to discuss and talk, because it means not taking the other person for granted. It means respecting the other as an individual and not making assumptions about each other. I like that, despite being together for so long, we have not melded to become one entity. I would really hate that. We are both still separate people with our own identity but working in partnership as a couple. I like this egalitarianism.

And so together, we have made the small and big decisions – like the one to remain child-free. Some people think child-bearing is a natural process of being a woman and motherhood, synonymous with womanhood. I have never felt that way. I have never felt the need to be a mother. When I look around and see women with children, I do not feel inadequate, nor do I feel I am missing out on something. Being a mother is a beautiful experience, I am sure, but it is not something every woman wants. I feel complete as I am.

From the very start of our relationship, I told you how I felt about not wanting to have kids. You understood me. You never made me feel any less of a woman and you never pressured me into changing my mind. We talked about it from time to time. And each time, we arrived at the same conclusion; we are happy without the need for children. The world is already so overpopulated as it is and we do not want to contribute to the growing numbers. We like the freedom that comes from being child-free.

In fact, not having kids means our union will always be founded on the very simple principle of two people committed to being together. There is nothing else forcing us to remain as a couple. This makes our marriage special. Thank you for respecting my views and understanding my feelings. Not every man would.

As I write this, I am also thinking about all the things we have gone through, all the ups and downs we have experienced. Where did all that time go? Just like that, in the blink of an eye, we have been married a decade.

I remember the day we got married. I was still recovering from my epic fall down the stairs when my feet went through the glass door. You came out of the shower to find me lying flat on my back, blood all over the kitchen floor. Just five minutes before, I had been on the phone making arrangements for our small wedding ceremony. That was the first medical emergency we experienced together. A week later, we got married, with me in a wheelchair.

The second medical emergency was nearly four years ago in Berlin. This time, it was a lot scarier. For the first time, I thought I was going to lose you. That ride to the Charité Hospital was possibly the longest 10-minute drive in my life. I did not know what was wrong with you. You were in so much pain and there was nothing I could do to help. In the Emergency Room, they whisked you away and as the door closed behind you, I was suddenly alone with the thought I could possibly never see you again. It was at that moment I understood the depth of how much you mean to me. How my world would be utterly hollow without you.

Finally, hours later, a nurse told me you would have to undergo surgery. We spent 12 days in Berlin with you in hospital. I was worried each time I had to leave you. You looked so weak and shrunken. Each time I left, I feared you would have a relapse while I was gone for the night. Remember the other patient in the ward suffering the same illness? He had been in hospital for two months and because they were not from Berlin, his wife was only able to visit him on weekends. The day they rolled him out of his room for his second surgery, his wife could not be there. I saw the worry in his eyes as his stretcher went past us. I did not want that to happen to us! What if you had to stay on longer in hospital while I had to return to Singapore for work?

I thought a lot about us as I walked around Berlin on my own. It was getting colder and the days were getting shorter. Nightfall comes early in Berlin in October. The chill of autumn was starting to bite and I had never felt more alone in my life. I thought about the recent disagreements we had. I could not even remember what they were about. Probably stupid things that did not even matter now. I thought about how this medical emergency was the wake-up call I needed to re-prioritise; how I must make more time and space for the people I love. I promised myself then I would stop putting work above everything else. Was it worth it to be constantly chasing deadlines if the people I love the most are not the people I prioritise?

Much of 2018 was spent with you in recovery. I was so grateful when we were able to spend a few months away from everything, just to recalibrate our lives, and make plans for our future.

Covid-19 has made this separation even more frustrating than before. It has driven home the point, for the second time for me, how fragile and fleeting life is. It has made us realise even our best-laid plans can suddenly be thrown asunder.

I really do not want us to be physically separated anymore. Life is so much more fun when you are around. Time passes so quickly and every moment we waste being apart is a moment lost, never to be found again. I plan for us to be together for a long time to come. It was in that period in Berlin, when I was contemplating the worst, that I realised how much we complete each other.

Je t'aime beaucoup, mon amour.

With all my love,
Shirlene

By day, SHIRLENE NOORDIN runs Phish Communications, a PR and digital agency. She also moonlights as a butler to her four senior cats – Orange, Teddy Bear, Ziggy and Loulou. She has recently discovered the joys of baking and now bakes sweet and savoury tarts in her free time. She is also reconnecting with her Malay heritage by researching into and cooking up traditional recipes from across the Nusantara region.

This Pain of Living in Exile

MD Sharif Uddin

Dear Jinnat,

It has been 13 years since I have been away from you. And this year has been the most difficult and painful. As the invasion of the coronavirus intensified, I often felt like I was heaving my last breath. Only the Creator knows how much terror I have gone through, the loneliness that gripped me in the pitch darkness of a small room. I repeatedly prayed to Him to keep me alive because I want to spend my last moments with you. I want to say goodbye to the world while holding your hand.

I vividly remember the first time you said goodbye to me at the airport. You looked at me in disgust, shrugged your shoulders and said: "Men do not have to be so broken. You have to be tougher." My courage grew when I heard your words. No one had ever told me to be brave like you did. But when the plane took off that day, there was a cry inside my chest. I cried. I cried. I cried.

It was so different when I first told you I would go abroad to work. You hugged me like a small child and repeatedly forbade me to. But when I presented reality to you, you agreed. Still, I often saw you crying silently. How hard you tried to hide your feelings! But we could not talk much – we just held each other's hands. Your throat would become dry whenever you spoke. I would change the subject, pretend everything was normal. I would tell stories to make you laugh. But you would turn away when tears welled up in your eyes and I pretended not to see.

How we had looked forward to our beautiful future plans! I thought I would come back with enough capital to start a small business. But whenever I wanted to return for good, more financial woes would appear – a huge wall of obstacles. It is not possible to break through this wall. The dream I had promised you seems to be getting harder and harder to fulfil as the days go by. Sometimes, one day seems like a century to me.

Today is the 15th year of our marriage. I have a lot of dreams for today. I thought I would go with you to see the lofty mountains over the roofs of Sylhet. It is a wonderful sight! When the sky is clear, the clouds cover the mountain like white sheets. When it rains heavily, the huge mountain gradually becomes invisible. The first time I saw that scene, I felt like I was in heaven. That day, I knew I wanted to take you there one day. The two of us will spend time at the foot of the mountain.

But this is only a dreamer's dream. You are not given the chance to experience it. This failure is entirely mine. The time for a man to spend with his wife is lost, and I am in a daze without you. I keep losing focus at work. Your face, shaped like a betel leaf, appears again in my mind's eye.

Over 15 years of marriage, we have only spent two of those years together. Even though I have gone home on vacation a few times, the time we had spent was not a normal life at all. Every time I leave for Singapore, there is the same frustration and dissatisfaction.

Do you remember the first two years of our marriage? We wanted to be close to each other every moment. Every morning, the fragrance of love would fill our small house. We would be drunk without drinking. Drunk to be close to each other. Time spent with you was the best time of my life. There was a rhythm every day. When I returned home with a body tired from the day's work, all the fatigue would go away when I saw you. Your eyes would sparkle with joy at getting close to me. I, too, would forget my sweaty body and go insane to find you. The storm would blow between us. I would have been thrilled to fall in love with you all over again. At that time, we did not know how much distance the Creator had prepared for us!

We know this distance today. I live under the same sky as you but I cannot touch you even for a moment. Dear, I miss your warmth terribly. I miss the feeling of putting my head on your chest in the softness of the morning.

This dream city of Singapore is a sad city for me. The income of migrant workers increases at the speed of a tortoise. It has taught me to be civilised but not expect anything from its heart. Changes are made in the city port, but not in the dormitories of captive workers like me. People do not see the great suffering of the workers. At the end of the year, they enjoy their new homes, cars and a new life. Those who are afflicted with hardships are left behind.

This city has made me a money-making machine. It has taught me how to adapt day after day. It has enabled me to live life according to strict rules. This city has conditioned me to ignore both sun and rain. It has caused me to forsake loved ones for the sake of cash. It does not feel the emptiness of my heart as it has sucked up all the affection, tenderness and love in me like a hungry creature. It has made me inanimate.

But this city also has its good things. It is surrounded by water and filled with green forests. People from all over the world have come and settled in this city of eternal summer. Life here is orderly and dynamic with the modernity of technology. In this city, the cries of the cuckoo and the solemn rhythm of mechanical life merge in the afternoon. In exchange for my sweat, this city becomes more modern.

But in this exile, I am alone. The small window next to my bed defines my loneliness. Standing there, I see the sky. I get up in the middle of the night to hear the sound of rain. I have no one here. No one asks if I am well. No one asks what food I would like. Or someone who says: Let's go somewhere fun today. My day is spent in the sun and rain and my night in a closed 3m x 12m room.

House arrest. I do not know when I will be released.

There is no one to watch over me when I am sick and have to stay in bed. When everyone goes to work, the loneliness in the room catches me. Then the body fights with the mind. You have to handle everything yourself. You may forget to eat. I lay numb in bed. No one will come to help even when

I shout out. Being ill in exile seems like a cursed life. I feel as if I have to atone for some unknown sin.

But I still have to survive. You have to survive in order to survive. You have to live with hope. You have to live with dreams. You have to live by dreaming. You and me. Then I become greedier for survival. I forget all self-loathing.

I know you are having a hard time reading what I write. But this is the reality. Seeing my cheerful smile, you may think I am feeling good, though I know how incomplete I am without you.

From time to time, a pair of sparrows come and spend time at the corner of my window. Seeing them, my mind dances with joy. My imagination makes me more anxious to be close to you. Sometimes, when I wake up, I will see you sitting next to me! The strong smell of jasmine is on you. Raise your hand and touch my forehead! Let your pink lips rest on my intoxicated mouth! I close my eyes in disbelief and open them to test your presence. I long to hear you say: "Hurry, get up. Let us walk barefoot on the dew-drenched grass!"

A simple life in exile. A life bound in invisible chains.

But this pain of living in exile is also a wonderful chapter. Every day, I need to tell you something from that chapter, so you know how I spend my moments without you. In this letter, every word will touch your heart. It will end any misunderstandings. You will have no hatred for me. You will not feel neglected. In fact, you will be more eager to get to me, hug me tightly, love me intensely. I know you will close the door and cry when you finish reading this letter.

Jinnat, I spend my days with old memories.

Like your worried look when I had a slight fever. How you had cooked different types of healing food for me. You did not sleep all night, thinking how you could make me feel better. You stroked my hair so gently my eyes would close comfortably. And when I awoke, you were still stroking my hair the same way. You wanted to take all my illnesses into yourself.

I used to gaze at you when you slept on my chest at night. I would kiss your forehead. Who knew I would be a strange lover for you? When I wonder how this silly, sweet girl would be alone without me, I cannot sleep all night. I feel guilty. I think I am cheating on you.

Jinnat, the seed of love that you sowed in the garden of my heart long ago has turned into a tree today. Every moment, I feel its cool shadow. I feel your love for me. I believe you are alive. You are alive and breathing.

Sometimes, I feel I have to end my life in exile and come home to you. Our world will become colourful again. Under a full moon, I will spread the carpet on the roof. And in the light of the brown dawn, we will walk barefoot on the dew-soaked grass with our hands entwined. I, in a red Punjabi suit and you, in your blue sari. There will be music. We two will be drunk on the scent of hasna henna blossoms.

Be well, my dear. I pray I may return to you with a healthy body very soon. One day, we will be back together. We will exchange love again.

Your Sharif

MD SHARIF UDDIN is from Bangladesh and currently works in the piling and construction sector as a safety coordinator. His short stories and poems have been published in journals and anthologies in Singapore and Bangladesh, including *Migrant Tales*. His poem, "A Worker's Journey", was shortlisted in the 2014 Migrant Worker Poetry Competition. *Stranger to Myself*, his first book, won the 2018 Singapore Book Awards for non-fiction title. The sequel, *Stranger to My World: The Covid Diary of a Bangladeshi Migrant Worker*, was published in 2021.

Tacit in the Air

Hernie Mamat

There is a lingering chill in the air. Unseasonably cool, in spite of it being August. I pull the cashmere cardigan around me a little tighter and rearrange the hastily-tied bow on my side. Would not want to accidentally catch a cold now, just a matter of days before the flight. I smile at the thought of long, balmy evenings, leisurely dinners and fancy tuk-tuk sightings. Although I know the minute we land, we will whinge about how swelteringly hot it is. How long has it been? I cannot even remember, in spite of it being always at the top of my special cities list. Was not always the case though, especially when I had to engage with it under totally different circumstances then.

Let's start with the year of your departure. The end as we knew it. As you pack, I try to help but my heart is not in it. I leave you to it and contemplate what living on my own will be like, with only the cats for company. I am already overthinking. As always, you would say. I relish the idea of having the house to myself, having more time for myself and the luxury of not having to consider anyone else's needs but my own. Simultaneously, however, the feeling rings suspiciously hollow, as if I am trying to cram a void with as many things as I can in order to avoid or deny the obvious. I shake my head to no one in particular. Plenty of time to contemplate that, I think. The ride to the airport feels leaden and I half-wish I am not there. After all, what is the point of saying goodbye at the airport? Futile really, no? I attempt to not look or sound plaintive. We wave and promise to call every day. And that was that.

Three weeks later, I am on a plane Bangkok-bound. As the wheels are lowered and announcements are heard overhead, I wonder if it would be awkward. We hug, exchange kisses. I am embarrassed to admit it but it warms the cockles of my ageing heart you seem truly happy to see me. We set off into the gritty reality of the city on a Friday evening, replete with traffic, smog and errant drivers. But for us, it is a splendid moment.

All too soon, I am the one packing, arranging for a car, anxiety creeping in my veins, worrying about everything. I leave today and I think about how many more times I will have to experience this. A long depressing car-ride later, glass and steel envelope me while muzak fills the air. My heart cleaves. Around me, tired faces, people coming and going to who-knows-where places. I see a man with a towel over his head. Skin weather-beaten and paper-thin. And I wonder if he has someone to go home to. Someone who will greet him at the door as if it is the first time. Always. Someone who will plant a heavy kiss on his lips. Someone who will embrace him tightly and make him feel that even though the world is going to the dogs, just for that moment, all is right. Someone who makes him feel he has an anchor to life that is so grounded and real that he should never ever doubt.

Four weeks later, I am on a plane Bangkok-bound. Have you ever noticed the viscidity of the air in that city? It clings to your clothes, your hair, your skin. It is an inescapable feature, some say, a part of its charm. Much like its faintly recognisable smell. Not quite fetid, a heady mix of exhaust fumes, near-rancid oil and fish sauce. And so, my tango with the city begins. The heat and dust are oppressive. Being in a taxi feels dangerous. I know no one. I understand nothing. Words and signs are indecipherable. I return to the empty apartment and wait for you to return. You are delayed. I sulk. For that moment, we accept our internecine existence. Eventually, I relent and we begin the evening. We talk about everything and nothing. I leave the next day. My heart cleaves. One thinks one gets used to it. But one doesn't.

Six weeks later, I am on a plane Bangkok-bound. The wall of sultry air meets me at the entrance as a form of greeting. At gate 5, I spy the car and wave. The driver disembarks, says: "Hello, Madam! No luggage?" I shake my head and get into the car as he holds the door open for me. I sink back as I welcome the air-conditioning on high. As the vehicle moves away, I anticipate its twists and turns, and recognise instantly the landmarks which dot the ride along, with the long expanses of nothing but asphalt. The ride is uneventful. No road blocks, no congestion, no diversion due to a royal motorcade. The sprawling urban landscape comes into view and soon enough, I spy the tall white, now-familiar building. I disembark and take pleasure from the scent of petrichor.

And so it goes, the constant movement and exploration of this metropolis and of each other. We navigate around ourselves in the same way as we manoeuvre its grid lines. Sometimes in a desultory fashion, but more often than not, like a hound after a scent. Constantly, we are surprised by what we, and it, have to offer, with its multitudes of conurbation. On one occasion, we head to the suburbs to explore a creative space and find ourselves facing an old Lockheed passenger airplane. Magnificent and imposing and such a sight to behold in the otherwise nondescript environs. Its hushed interiors now housing a posh cocktail bar and an even posher restaurant. In another quarter, a smiling giant dog stood, four metres high, as people of various ilk and ages jump up and down for a photo. I catch an old woman's eye as we both witness the scene in amusement. She smiles and my face follows hers by way of example as the corners of my mouth find themselves turning up. No words are needed. Collectively, the mutual non-understanding of the silliness is enough. I reflect momentarily the extraordinariness of a place that can throw up such moments of awe, joy and surprise in its nooks and crannies.

The city gives us a sense of liberty. We feel free to be ourselves, and more than ourselves. We glide on the streets, keenly aware of the city pulsating unabashedly in all its imperfect glory. This occasionally includes waiting 20 minutes for the traffic light to change from red to green and then have the green remain green for only 30 seconds. But if you seek, this is also the city which offers those who are persevering enough to discover its plethora of finds in its labyrinthine streets and myriad alleyways. Opportunities for one to go

"Oh!", and savour a new-found delight.

A familiar routine develops and my concept of what home means morphs, evolves, coalesces, opens itself up to possibilities. In my now frequent jaunts, alone and together with you, my lenses have changed, adapted, become less syncopated. We nod, we smile, grateful for the sheer effort at the attempt to understand as opposed to chasing and chasing for absolute understanding or to be completely understood. In this city, the human exchange is palpable.

Four weeks later, you are on a plane Singapore-bound. We exchange many messages while you are waiting to board and make jokes about the culture shock bound to strike you upon arrival. A few hours on, I am waiting in the cool sanitised air, thinking I can almost taste the chlorine. My arms are crossed. You emerge. You say: "Another usual position." It is an inside joke, as many things are in this rapport we have built, nursed and nurtured over 16 years. We head to the taxi stand where a man is reciting lane numbers as if his life depended on it. We are ushered through speedily. "Welcome back," I say. You nod. No further words are needed.

Weekends such as these pass in a blur, as if life is on fast-forward and teeming with white noise. We become hermits long before anyone has whispered the word "pandemic" or fathomed its impact on life around the world. At times vituperative, others cloyingly sweet, we traverse each other, remembering, remembering, always remembering. Because it never pays to forget. I am a big believer in serendipity. A concatenation of events. When everything that happens is a matter of confluence, aligned stars and kismet. When we first met, that is exactly how it felt and even though our chosen arrangement occasionally raises sceptical eyebrows, our lives are not yet equal to the sum of its potential parts.

You leave the next day. My heart cleaves. One thinks one gets used to it. But one doesn't. Still. The first day is always the hardest. An ache resides, tangible as anything I can reach out and touch. I have delayed washing the sheets. The sharp vinegary tang from the T-shirt you wore while gardening wafts not so gently from the top of the laundry pile. I keep the room door shut so that Tacit hangs in the air. Just so that for the briefest of time, I am content. Content being able to breathe you in. To inhale you until there are no traces left. Time passes, filled with a series of expected, anodyne activities, but I cannot help thinking life has an ersatz quality to it. Two weeks later, I am on a plane Bangkok-bound.

"I have decided. I am quitting. In January," you say. How odd life is, you think. That cliché about expecting the unexpected truly does happen. Only not to you, you thought once. In the background, the fetching news broadcaster is muttering something about Wuhan. The words "virus" and "death" quickly follow. Selfishly, I think an illness far away from me does not concern me in the least. At that moment, I have more pressing concerns and I pause to think about how I should respond to your announcement without sounding callous. I recall the living apart. I remember the years of being separated. I reminisce already the smoky jazz bar at the end of what has become "our" very long street in a city we have grown to know and love. The city that ironically has been the catalyst for our reawakening. Various images surface in my mind's eye, in full technicolour glory, the proverbial urban jungle, relentless in its fecundity. What will happen to all that?

"Did you say March?"

I am a big believer in serendipity. The months of government-mandated separation gives me time to breathe. I tell myself I am being stoic. But I know it is because a part of me just needs to get used to the idea your socks will again be where I do not want them. My head is churning out diverse permutations, illustrating scenarios, domestic and otherwise. I am not ashamed to think it. I have learned to enjoy the quiet time. The unalloyed joy of independence. The fact that I can do yoga day or night or both. Eat or don't eat. Work for the whole day because I need to or I feel like it. I catch myself thinking about what I would lose or the compromises I would need to make when we live under the same roof again. But I suppose, part of being an over-thinker involves driving yourself round the bend in a loop of what-ifs.

But then 11pm comes along. We talk about everything and nothing. About the cats. About the fact we will have four cats soon. About how our preferred dining spots are struggling to stay afloat in the midst of this contagion and if they can survive long enough to remain open. About your brother and how he is managing in a lockdown ala Parisien (Parisian). About our friends who have invited me many times to Zoom parties and how I have resolutely declined each time. About your more recently-minted friends and how you all cook for each other almost daily. There is a sense of community. I tell you this seemingly simple kindness is profound in its humanity. I tell you about how, over the Easter weekend, I found two eggs in a nest in the bougainvillea tree in the back garden laid by a Bulbul. How more apt could that be? The next evening, I complain about empty shelves in the supermarket and express my disbelief that mustard has been sold out for two whole weeks. We discuss the politics and antics of politicians and non-politicians alike and lament our now-cancelled European trip.

In these nightly talks, I am reminded how we have persisted and thrived. How, in our own ways, we know exactly what to say or what not to say but say it anyway. How we can finish each other's sentences or how you think you know what I am thinking and are usually right. Usually. Occasionally, we slip, cut ourselves to shreds, and create bulwarks to protect our egos before tearing them down as we fly the white flag. We lick our lacerations and say sorry, even though we both know history repeats itself. For these and a million other things, we realise our lives are inextricably linked. So much so that where I end, you begin. We are a Möbius loop, you and I. We are not part of each other's lives. You are my life and I am yours.

And so, begrudgingly, I clear the cupboard space I have colonised. I catch myself thinking about what you would lose or the compromises you would need to make when we live under the same roof again.

Einstein once said people have it all wrong. That men fall in love and expect the woman to never change. And that women fall in love in expectation of change. Ultimately, everyone is disappointed. Perhaps that is why we have survived this thing called life, complete with all its vicissitudes, trials and tribulations. Our only expectation is that we be the best version of ourselves. And so, no matter how flawed we are – and oh, how terribly flawed we are – I would like to think we will live the rest of our lives together as a constant work in progress, a perennial labour of love.

HERNIE MAMAT has a long-standing love for everything literary. For this, she credits her mother who created a personal library for her at home, making sure she never did not have a book to read. Having cultivated her ardency for words from a very young age, she went on to study literature throughout her school years. Since then, she has combined her twin loves for literature and teaching and was instrumental in initiating and developing various curricula, including Arts Appreciation and Creative Writing. Currently, she is a senior lecturer at Temasek Polytechnic and part of the communication skills team.

Love Where We Live

Fann Sim

Dear Markus,

As I write this, we are 10,252km apart, a numerical constant that represents the longing in my heart. This time, it is you I pine for while I am in Singapore with my dying father.

A cancer called mesothelioma is about to consume him fully and take him away from us. I see the physical changes in my father and I cannot fathom how small he can become until he dies.

Every day, he eats a little less food, takes a little more morphine. He spends more and more time away in his opioid-induced haze and less time awake.

On our first trip to Singapore since the Covid-19 pandemic, I said to you I needed to stay so I do not feel guilty for being away. When my father dies, I cannot imagine not grieving by my mother's side. You understood and agreed to this arrangement, despite being a new dad to our daughter,

Mae, who was eight months old then. That was my parents' first time meeting her.

Before that trip was over, we made the prudent decision for you to return alone to Munich to pack up our flat and end the lease. No point keeping it if Mae and I are going to be in Singapore for an indefinite period. We did not know how much time my father has left nor how severe his condition is, except that it is terminal.

In any case, we had barely woven ourselves into Munich and had few ties there.

When you went back to Germany, you had also spent some time with your mother in Frankfurt. I hope that had alleviated, to some extent, how isolating it must have felt back in our own home.

People tell me I am filial to my father and brave to take on Mae's day-to-day caregiving single-handedly, but the hardest thing for me is putting our young marriage on hold. I could not have done it without your assurance. I miss you so much. I am holding onto the thought of our reunion as the light at the end of this very long and windy tunnel.

But in the same way I evade feelings of guilt by being here for my father, a different guilt brews in me for taking our daughter away from you. Guilt has a way of dreaming up harsh realities in the mind, and logic and prudence cannot triumph over the simple fact I am here while you are there.

In that moment of joy and excitement to finally be reunited with my family again, we never expected we would not be returning back together. On the day you left Singapore for Munich, I was overwhelmed with insecurity and self-loathing. How could I have chosen my father over you?

We continue to live in uncertainties of a Covid-19-infested world and separation in a time like this feels like forever. We had made plans to reunite but they would always be made tenuous on the whims of the sneaky virus.

Over the last six months, you had missed: Mae's first "Papa", first birthday, first step, first word ("Dogggg," she said when we saw a goldie while out on a hike), and her first toddler tantrum. Nothing can make up for missing these firsts. Nothing can allow us to revel in these milestones together in the same space.

You missed the bloom of her character, how curious and sociable she is, brought out by being around my boisterous family.

All of a sudden, she seems to have left her babyhood in the dust and is now thick into her first year as a toddler. She is no longer the helpless, floppy blob you once rocked to ease.

One time when Mae and I were at the doctor's to get her scheduled shots, she became hysterical with tears. The doctor said she is at the age when she is competent in making memories.

I wondered at that moment if her memories of you are only as a face flat on my phone because that is all she has seen of you since you left. This has likely popped up in your mind as well but we have never talked about it. It is too painful for me.

I do not know how I can ever make it up to you.

***

Berlin

It was the start of the summer of 2016 when we first met in Berlin.

The first time we went out was to the annual *Karneval der Kulturen*, which has its roots as a political protest against xenophobia. Over four days, a part of Berlin transforms into a parade of street parties, food stalls, mobile music and theatre performances celebrating tolerance and cultural pride.

It is hard to put it into words the effect Berlin has on a person. In my experience, there is a carefree, experimental air to it that makes a person feel invisible. It was just what I needed after burnout from adulting and chronic job stress.

The invisibility I had felt in Berlin also let me feel there were not people watching me and watching us. Around me, casual racist and sexist judgments were passed far too freely and it made me afraid to explore a relationship construct like ours. I know, because I have heard my parents spew the same poison, intentional or not.

Over the course of summer, we had spent a lot of time on hikes, at lakes, and visiting museums cultivating this relationship. Falling in love felt so adult and easy this time around. Our conversations and experiences invigorated and nourished me like a tree planted by the water. Your humour and intellect drew me in.

Towards the end of our first summer together, we went to a music festival in Zurich with friends. You may not know this; I was myself not aware we were thought of as a couple until friends started to refer to you as my boyfriend. I guess we are together then?

My favourite "our thing" in Berlin was to go to Abirams, near your flat in Kreuzberg, late at night for soup. Do you remember the moment we figured out the restaurant was run by twins only after patronising it for almost three years? We were so tickled by that.

All summer romances have a turning point. Ours came in the form of me leaving Berlin to finish my final year as a graduate school student and we had to have the difficult talk of going long-distance. In the lead-up to it, I remember feeling constantly and physically sick to my stomach and would cry thinking about the seemingly nebulous future. I did not know if this was going to be a stereotypical summer fling or grow into something more.

You assured me by allowing me to talk, listening to and validating my anxieties.

After we said our temporary goodbyes, you consistently sent me postcards. They never contained words or written expressions of love but had drawn comics or figures. I recognise that perhaps your preference to show love is not through verbalising your love – as is mine. I have been quick to accuse you of being emotionally unavailable when you cannot meet me in my love language and for this, I am sorry.

The correspondence had an effect on my parents. It won them over and they began to adore you, even without having met you.

Those days with you in Berlin are one of the happiest periods of my life. It was just the two of us.

***

Munich

From what we know of distance, the jump from Berlin to Munich could be seen as a game of hopscotch.

It was anything but.

What the two of us had installed when we moved in together in the summer of 2019 has now been torn down by you a mere two years later. Over the last few months while apart, you have solitarily and heroically packed up the contents of our marital home, mended the physical markings we made on the rented property, and restored the flat to its vacant state.

Our first home on Wundtstrasse had a south-facing balcony we had lovingly decorated with a pallet couch, planters of sunshine-resistant lavenders and cosmos, and a big yellow umbrella. In the summer, we would spend evenings with a small barbecue, just the two of us. In the winter, you would go out first thing in the morning for a hit of the crisp, stabbing cold air to awaken your senses.

One of my favourite memories of our first home is you on the balcony, sitting on that pallet couch cradling our precious Mae when she was just a few days old. You were both enjoying the first spot of spring sunshine – her first spring.

The balcony was also where we had our first meal when we "closed the distance" (a term used by long-distance relationship couples to describe moving in together). In the span of our five-year relationship (three in courtship, two in marriage), we have spent almost half apart.

We moved to Munich because of your work and we were both fresh transplants to the city with no real connections or community. We regularly felt lonely as a couple, and really only had each other for company.

It was a very challenging phase for me. When a person moves for another person, a lot of complex emotions are involved. I had several emotional outbursts during that time because I kept lapsing into a zero-sum mindset that you had gained a housewife and I had lost my life in Singapore. There was a lot of resentment.

The hardest part was the self-doubt from losing my identity, which was largely defined by my work as a journalist. I suddenly had no responsibilities or professional goals and ended up focused only on running our household.

I do not know how we rode this wave, but I suspect with honesty and grace. A lot of times, it felt like I was talking at you and you were quietly listening. Sometimes, when I became too emotional about the issue, my mind filled the silence with whatever I thought you were thinking. Talk to me!

Our flat felt like an oasis of comfort and familiarity from the provincial Bavarian folkway. Wundtstrasse represented a sweet and blissful new chapter for us. New marriage, new home, new baby.

We never got to say goodbye to the first home we had built together.

***

Singapore

It has been six months since we parted. I have found myself poring through a book titled *How to Not Hate Your Husband After Kids* that has been lying next to my pillow the last two months. I am looking for answers to questions that have popped into my mind after Mae arrived. Obviously, I do not hate you! Marital frustrations have come up and I would like to know how we can be better partners to each other.

But it is almost impossible to get any reading done with an Energiser bunny of a toddler and an ever-dinging iPhone screaming for attention. Part of those notifications are scanty messages between us: Poor attempts to stay involved in each other's lives while apart, and living in different time zones.

It feels like our marriage has stagnated in the last one and a half years by deprioritising our need for romance. Go for date nights, they say; but how do we do that in Munich in the pre-vaccine Covid-19 reality? It was hard to find someone we could trust with our infant, in a city where we had no family and a very small social circle made up of new parents like us.

Coming to Singapore has given me room to breathe because I can hand Mae over to my family whenever I need a mental break. I look forward to us utilising these babysitting offers and having child-free time to find ourselves again.

While we have always maintained the importance of mobility as a defining feature of our cross-national family, we are ready to plant roots somewhere that we can always go back to.

Now that we have Mae, we can now be regarded as the basic social unit of a nuclear family. This will open doors for us in Singapore, such as your right to apply to visit our family here for a longer period of time, as well as becoming eligible for subsidised public housing.

We tried our luck at the quarterly housing lotto and were fortunate enough to get a spot. While you were away, I had to go alone to the Housing Board's office to book our flat. It was a bittersweet feeling to cross this milestone alone.

At my father's last oncology appointment, his doctor said he has exhausted all palliative treatment options and recommends we allow time to do its bidding. The doctor can now tell us with certainty he has six months left, less if there are complications.

I see the cruel contrast of my father's frailty against our daughter's rapid growth. A life is nearing its conclusion while another is only just beginning. One stumbles excitedly, while the other limps along slowly.

It is very difficult for me to come home and talk about our future home to my father with his terminal diagnosis looming over us. He will not live to see us move in and watch our marriage and family grow and evolve with time.

It is difficult to comprehend the gravity of life. When I do so in bits and pieces, it stirs an emotional storm in me but I am anchored by the stabilising effect you have in my life, regardless of how far you are from me.

Marriage is at times challenging but we have moved through many of those tough moments, together or apart, with each other in mind. Your love gives me strength to work through difficulties I face.

This season has taken a toll on me. I am exhausted. I am wanting, curious, and waiting to reunite so that we can live our family life together. I will be ready for the next thing we stumble onto together.

Love,
Fann

FANN SIM is a former journalist who has lived in Berlin, Munich and St Petersburg. She has a broad intellectual curiosity in many areas. Currently, they are birth work and parenting.

Pre-Destined

Ann Li

Dear Ex-spouse,

Your engagement plans have been announced and your wedding plans are underway. I ask myself: "How do I feel about your upcoming marriage? I look deep inside myself for an emotion. Is there jealousy or resentment? Do I wish things could have been different and that we were still married? I had always thought we would be married forever; I imagined a white picket-fences life, growing old together, having the security of each other for company. Oh yes, we would bicker and fight over trivial matters but we would be comfortable in each other's company, enjoying our books or movies, doing old-people things together. Yes, I wanted that for my life. I had always wanted that.

However, that will not be us. That thread of connection between us has been cut. I am staring down at my future; days of being alone, and being lonely, await me. I feel anxious. Am I looking forward to endless nights of Netflix with a bag of popcorn for company? Did we not promise each other at the altar we would stay married forever, for better or for worse, till death do us part? I realise now that promise was never ever capable of being fulfilled.

Looking back, I wonder how I could have missed the signs? Very soon after the wedding, things started to change. Nothing I did was ever good enough. I was constantly criticised about everything – from how I dressed, to food that was not up to par, to my coming home late after a tough day at work. Even during the storm and I was stranded outside our home because you had taken my house keys, you ignored my phone calls and made no attempt to rush back to let me in. I watched the dark clouds envelope the sky as that afternoon turned to evening, tired from the day's work, fatigue brought on by pregnancy. How I longed for a warm drink and a lie-down.

Finally, you came back and when I got upset, you yelled at me. You told me I was not entitled to get angry; I was never to fight with you because you would always be stronger and louder. What monster had you turned into? I never suspected anything, your initial cruelty and withdrawal from me. I often wondered why you had pursued me in our teens, married me and then cast me aside almost immediately. You took every opportunity to spend time away from home. You planned your business trips to straddle weekends, even after the children came. I had wondered, but never asked. I thought I knew why. I was worthless, someone to be despised. There was nothing good about me. I was seriously flawed and not worthy of being loved. I recall during one mealtime, when you had been particularly mean; I asked you why you hated me so much. Then you looked at me and that look said everything; you had come to the realisation that you did abhor me, your eyes acknowledged it. I will remember that visage for life.

Then one day, you told me about Fred. You said you had a crush on him, but that was all. After our family Sunday lunch, you walked away to meet him as we left the restaurant, both your backs to me. I watched as you both chattered and laughed and made your way towards the waiting car, holding champagne bottles, an evening of fun awaiting you. At that moment, I felt as if someone had stabbed me in the heart, with scalpel-like precision, in one swift stroke, the deep cut, then the raw and relentless pain that followed. I held the hand of our child asking myself, what next? That scene of both your backs went on perpetual replay in my head. I felt spurned but my tears could not find a path down my cheeks; they were stuck in my throat and I trembled so badly. The pain in my heart. This time, I felt the pain in my tummy as well. A sharp pain. Was it our unborn child feeling it as well? What situation was he going to be born into? Would his dad love him? Be strong, be strong: I told myself as I had to keep it together for him. Did you ever think of that day? Soon after, I nearly miscarried but our son clung on for dear life. Did the sadness in me somehow permeate into his being?

After you and Fred broke up, you promised to try again. You wanted to have a family life. So, we played happy family a little longer. You convinced me you could change. I convinced myself you would change. I wanted to believe that. Now with our children, I was beginning to build my white picket fences again. However, that did not last very long. I started to notice things were once again not right. Your sudden change of plans on the eve of our family vacations. Your business trips with indefinite home arrival dates. I started to investigate and stalk you and that was when I found out about Ken.

You traded time with kids and family for weekends in Phuket. Your business trips spilled over into weekends spent with him. A flight to Koh Samui to surprise him on his birthday. I called you but you did not pick up the phone. I was going insane with jealousy. I saw that photo of him sitting on your lap leaning against you, holding hands. I had not seen a smile from you like that for a while. In that photo, you looked ecstatic. I was in shambles. When you love much, you are hurt so much more. I had started to heal from Fred but now there was Ken to open up those wounds again. Would I ever recover?

When your husband gives his heart, mind, soul, spirit and body to another, you can feel like your heart shattering into a thousand pieces. That was where I was. I could not imagine how I could mend those broken parts again. Loneliness can lead you to a very dark place. You find things to fill that void, and when those run out, that pain revisits you as an unwelcome guest. I tried so hard to excise it. However, I could not. In fact, I seemed to find more reasons to afflict myself. I was now obsessed. Every spare evening at home, I would wonder where you both were and what you were up to. I wished I could make myself invisible and tail you. I wanted to be able to see your secret love messages with each other. How could I break into your phone? What were you planning for the next evening? When I drew a blank, I tormented myself even more by imagining the most lurid thoughts I could conjure up.

When you eventually moved out, I hated you so much for abandoning me. I had to figure out parenting by myself. Slowly, I began to find my feet and I got on with life. Parent coffees, swimming lessons, homework, exams. I was on my own and I was determined to raise resilient and happy children. I did not want our son to be like you, I also did not want our daughter to be like me, a loser. I knew I had to shield my hurts from them. They needed both a father and a mother, albeit a dad at his convenience. They were to remain children and stay innocent and unaffected by the sadness that permanently resided at our home. The children, and I, were going to survive this.

As the years passed, you began to make more of an effort to spend time with the children. You tried, in your own way, to be an involved parent. We went on family trips, though we fought all the time. I began to see more of you and I recognised the effort you made. You became less critical of me and less explosive with the children. You transitioned from being absent to being very much present.

Through time, we found a rhythm to our interactions. I started to get used to your company again. This time, I no longer saw a monster but a caring person trying his best to make up for his absence, to be a dad and provider to the children, and a friend to me. Something had changed in you. You went about being a family man. You listened to all our struggles and empathised. You remembered birthdays and planned meals and events so we would not miss out on the city's exciting offerings. I saw and appreciated your efforts. I learnt to let go of the hurts and to forgive. I must confess it was initially a struggle. In my head, forgiving you meant you were without blame and I wanted to hold you to account. However, I knew I had to release you from my emotional prison. Forgiving you meant I was allowing myself to heal. In my wounded state, I had sought to blame you for everything. In my healing, I began to look outward, towards understanding you more. I told myself I could learn to love you again but this time, as a friend.

I do wonder often what you might have been going through all those early years. Perhaps there was a secret parallel world I was not privy to. The world you kept hidden and did not let anyone in. You were in there, day and night, fighting your demons. The self-loathing and guilt. Dealing with the wounds of your childhood, your own perception of being judged and being condemned. Struggling to find affirmation. For so long, as you were engaged in battling the phantoms of this hidden world, you were unable to deal with my feelings. Overwhelmed with the constant struggles, you could not expend any effort to care for the children. You were desperately trying to survive. You were trying to "fix" yourself. Meanwhile, the assault of contrasting interests competed to get your attention, your hurting spouse, your new love, your young vulnerable children, your family, and most importantly, you, your sanity. And in the mix of all these, the real world, life. You, too, were a victim. Sometimes, it feels like life sabotages all the little moments of happiness. Heavy hammers lurk round the corner to destroy little pieces of heaven we try to build for ourselves. Spoiling relationships, taking along precious lives with it, destruction of self-esteem. Unbeknown to both of us, we were fighting demons, not each other. We were each other's casualties, and the children suffered collateral damage.

Not too long ago, I looked at you and thought to myself you seemed genuinely happy. Had you healed? You were in a good place, I had to get there too. I spoke to my inner self; I told myself my identity was not tied to my marital status, to you or anybody else. I was first myself and I had to make sure I was whole. What defined me? My religion, my values, my children, my family, my experiences, both good and bad. My plans had been altered but I did not have to stop dreaming and aspire for other things. That was my reality, that you would not always be by my side. I was on my own now. I needed to learn to help myself. I started to learn from you, to focus on me and "fix" myself too. I am on that path right now. I sincerely hope in your darkest moments, in your loneliest moments, I did, in some way, manage to help and support you. I prayed every day for wisdom, composure, and a loving spirit. I prayed every day for healing for this broken heart of mine.

At the beginning of this journey, I regretted having met you. I wished so badly then I could turn back time and change my life choices. I am so glad I have departed from that place now. I guess this was the path circumscribed for us; we were predestined to marry and have our children together. Maybe at the end of our lives, when we are allowed to have a glimpse of our personal histories, we might be able to piece together the puzzle of our paths, why and where they crossed, merged, then separated, and perhaps we will know why it all happened that way. Even though it is still quite a maze to me, what I do know is the children were intended as gifts to us, in the darkest periods of my life, we were blessed with wonderful miracles. Out of the darkest, most difficult and saddest circumstances, God chose to give us these shining stars. We were inextricably bound from the beginning, before we met, before we came into existence in this world.

You will get married soon. I wish you both a blissful marriage. You deserve to find happiness. It had always been there; you just needed to clear your path and claim it. You may well have. I will too.

From your ex-wife,
Ann

ANN LI is a retired banking professional and is pursuing her life-long passion of working with the arts.

I Am My Own Woman

Amy Chia

I was packing to leave you when you jumped out of bed and punched the back of my head. When I fell to the floor, you went to the kitchen and came back with a knife. Shoving me into a corner, you drew the curtains and returned to kick me. Waving the blade in my face, you said something that would change me forever: "You are just a woman."

I begged for forgiveness and said I was wrong. You dropped the knife and played nice. You liked your woman to obey. As long as I never dared to leave, or angered you again, you promised to be good to me. Kneeling, you held my face and claimed you were sorry, but you loved me, and that was why I should never make mistakes again.

I sat on the toilet as the shower ran. Since you had forgiven me, you had allowed me to get presentable and go to work. Everywhere hurt; fortunately, nothing was broken. A small red bruise had bloomed on the side of my head; there were bigger, uglier spots on my thighs and arms where you had struck. I hid the bruises with clothing and cosmetics as I got ready to leave your house, pretending nothing had happened, lying I would be back with your dinner after work. When you stopped me, my heart pounded, and I almost gave the ruse away. You casually reminded me disciplining me was an act of love, so there was no need for anyone else to know, since we both would not like to see him get upset again.

I fled to my parents' house in a taxi. When my mother felt something was off, I lied I had had a fall and was on sick leave, mumbling she should not make a fuss. My parents would never have imagined what had happened. I dared not think about their reactions. I did not want to see them heartbroken. I hid under my childhood duvet, exhausted, and slept most of that day. Shortly after my parents turned in for the night, I made my way to the bathroom in the dark. My mother had left me a bowl of rice porridge on the dinner table with a note to warm it up before eating it. I sobbed in the shower as I scrubbed myself clean.

In those days more than two decades ago, to the advantage of cowards like you, help and support were not readily available for women. Going to the police would be like stepping into another hell. Good Chinese girls in their mid-20s were expected to walk down the aisle with stable partners; if not, they would be dismissed as flawed or unmarriable by 30. Good Chinese girls would never have met bad boys and gotten themselves beaten up. If they did and made a fuss, they risked being blamed and shamed, bringing their family's reputation down with them. Good Chinese girls were supposed to be living picture-perfect lives.

***

Work became a safe haven and my efforts paid off. About a year after I left you, the digital consultancy I had been working in, assigned me to a three-month project with a client in Hong Kong. It was the new millennium, a fresh century had started, and I jumped at the chance to be as far away as I could get from you. The city was my first overseas posting and the cosmopolitan island lived up to its flashy neon reputation. My time was mine, and I invested every waking minute between two great loves – growing my pay cheque and partying. Overseas stint, nightlife, and Hong Kong. Check. Check. Check!

At beer o'clock sharp, I was already at my favourite bar in Causeway Bay, singing along to the chorus of "Lady Marmalade" with the live band and getting my buzz from B-52 shots. But no, it was still too soon to *voulez-vous coucher* with the hottie bartender. I could lick the salt trail off his washboard abs, down the shot of tequila in the valley of his bulging pecs and suck the slice of lemon between his eager lips. Just not the happy ending. Not with the bartender, not with any guy. Like you, they could all seem nice – until they were not.

***

The movie *Titanic* was released around Christmas of 1997. Like many young women then, I had harboured dreams of meeting my own Jack, someone who would do anything for me. I would *just know* he was the soulmate I was searching for. He would see *me* beneath the persona I showed the world. But unlike the tragic ending in the movie, we would get to live our happily-ever-after, go on adventures in every corner of the world, locking hands and sailing into candy-pink sunsets. A life with someone I love, an ordinary miracle for an ordinary girl. *How naive.* I changed my dream when I fled from you two years ago. In 2002, at the age of 26, I no longer needed to have someone to complete my world. In my new future, I would be solo on the hull of my own *Titanic*.

But on a clear evening later that year, in front of a real sunset, a boy stood nervously next to me by the railings of the newly gentrified Fullerton Bay, where fancy restaurants had just sprouted up and lovers lingered after dinner. The boy had asked me out on a date with the shyness of 20-year-olds, reserved a table for two after asking what I would prefer, taken care to button up his shirt and arrived earlier to wait for me.

We had noticed each other at a club where he had worked as a part-time DJ and mixed cocktails. In time, he had learned the songs I liked and would introduce me to new favourites. I started looking forward to how he would look up as I arrived, as if he had been waiting for me. Half-Japanese and half-Chinese, he was beautiful, even more so now with the orange light of dusk dancing on his face. He was only 21, as fresh and gentle as the evening breeze cooling my cheeks. I had started calling him H-*chan*, the way the Japanese people affectionately addressed children.

As he smiled, his eyes sparkled and curved into crescent moons, and I smiled back at him. This boy had so grown on me that I wanted to be a little brave, I wanted to go on this date and give him closure in person. He did not deserve the callous way I would catch and release other guys for sport.

If only I still believed in soulmates. If only I had met him before you hit me. But I did not tell him that despite my seemingly strong façade, I was not fine. I was still crying, trapped in recurring night terrors of being hurt by you.

Instead, I made up an excuse that five years was too much of an age gap, that he was too young for me. *We could be friends for a longer time.* H-*chan* had his whole life stretched out in front of him, clean as a sheet of paper. He could do better than me, like how I could have done better than you. As I waited for the sun to fall under the sea and for hope to slip away between us, I found myself praying for time to turn back. If you had never existed in my life and robbed me of my hopes and dreams, and if I could have fallen in love with someone, that someone would have been H-*chan*.

***

Another unfamiliar room, a familiar throbbing in my head, an unpleasant recollection of throwing up somewhere along Club Street to usher in Christmas Day, the broad, naked, shoulders of a hook-up next to me. Untangling myself from the mess of strange sheets, I shimmied into my clothes and snuck out of his studio. These casual encounters had no ties to undo later, and I was free to leave whenever I wanted. You had taught me never to trust men.

Outside, the air was dewy fresh and early birds were chirping with gusto to greet the dawn. I lighted a cigarette and enjoyed the calm after the ruckus that is usually Christmas Eve. The street was decorated with technicolour confetti that had spilled out of various bars the night before. Save for the grumbling road sweeper who was cleaning up the after-party, I was alone.

I could not wait for the festive hullaballoo to be over. I would be taking off to Seoul for work and then to Bali for massages. Footloose and fancy-free, I could travel independently and at short notice. I did not mind my career was taking off and taking over most of my 30-year-old life. The freedom to go wherever I wished, to live whichever way I wanted, came with climbing up salary bands. There is an old saying in Teochew: "When you lean on a mountain, it will collapse. When you count on a man, he will run."

***

Okinawa was a two-hour flight from Shanghai, where I was based for work. H-*chan* was cycling around Japan and we had arranged to meet for the weekend on the island, surrounded by sake-clear waters. On the first day, we cycled around town together. Whenever I lagged haplessly behind, I would childishly brake in the middle of the path, refusing to budge. Each time, he simply cycled back, patiently waiting for me to heave forward. The trip marked 10 years of our friendship. During those years, he had become a listening ear, a shoulder to lean on, a warm bowl of rice porridge when I needed to be fragile. The trust you had destroyed when you laid your punches on me in the name of love, H-*chan* used 10 years of friendship to rebuild it.

On our second day in Okinawa, we decided to take a bus to the famed Churaumi Aquarium. It was at the massive Kuroshio tank that I met the first whale sharks and manta rays of my life. I stood speechless, gawking at these gentle giants flying in the water, imagining how it would be like to meet one of them in their natural habitat. Even after returning to Shanghai, after the post-holiday spring in my gait turned into day and night shuffling on the work mill, I could not get rid of the desire to meet these amazing creatures out in the blue. The sea was calling, and I had to go.

***

Diving taught me to be calm, to keep breathing and look towards the sun. I have been diving with a regular group of friends from Spain, France, and Germany for the last 10 years. Each year, we would vote on the next destination, and they would gamely travel halfway around the world to Asia. For our group's 8th year, we picked the Tubbataha National Reefs Park, a scuba diving sanctuary in the middle of the Sulu Sea in the Philippines. Tubbataha had been on my diving bucket list for a long time.

From Manila Airport, we connected to a domestic flight to the Palawan archipelago, travelled onward to the pier at Puerto Princesa in rickety vans, and sailed on a live-on-board boat for nine more hours to get there. The best places for diving, much like the best moments and people in life, are worth going out of the way for. There is no habitable land on the national park, the boat with the vast sea surrounding us would be where we would rest our feet and fins. These couple of weeks each year as we floated far away from civilisation were special as we reconnected, met some big fish, kept each other alive in whipping currents under water, and went off the grid together as soulmates of a connected sea.

On the last night, I signed up for a massage on the upper deck. I was not sure if it was all that diving that aided the masseuse or her very determined elbows and thumbs that finally released the knots in my shoulders. I was annoyed when the treat ended, and I had to wake up. But as I opened my eyes, I found myself wrapped in a glittering snow globe. In the night, the sea and the sky blended and stretched out in an orb that circled the boat. Up as high and as far as my eyes took me, scintillated thousands and thousands of stars, thousands of years away, yet so near it felt like I could pluck them out from the night.

The Milky Way, reflected on the surface of the sea, so complete in her allure, she made me feel centred again. I spent a long time lying down on the hull alone, lulled by the gentle sway of the boat, listening to the swishing rhythm of the waves, letting the playful breeze caress my skin, spellbound under the miracle of this star-washed night. I realised then, that the pain you had inflicted, had finally passed.

***

I never saw you again, though I still remember your wretched face as you waved the knife at me. I remember enough to point out where the bruises were on my body, and how many days they took to fade from indigo to ochre to sand. These scars have become a part of my memory. But much more vividly than the old scabs they had become, I remember every city I have been to and lived in, thanks to a fulfilling career that has indulged my wanderlust. I log every scuba diving adventure, from being on the ocean floor with circling great white sharks at the Neptune Islands of Australia, to looking for 10-foot-long blue marlins at Yonaguni where the fiery sun sets on Japan. Each world under the sea brings me incredible serenity and joy. I have opened myself up, met and made friends from three continents, many of whom I carry in my heart.

When I am in Singapore, I sleep soundly through the night in my own apartment, a happy place where I am surrounded by books and many favourite things. The door is always open to friends who come over to celebrate birthdays or just hang out and chitchat. I am gaining weight as I hole up at home, discovering creative writing, enthusiastically preparing to go back to art college for a second postgraduate degree, a brand-new adventure that makes my heart hum. I am growing fonder of my parents as we grow older together. The nephews I had once cradled when they were infants, now play mobile games with me, huddled under my childhood duvet in the same room my parents had kept for me in their house.

The days after what you did to me were long and cold as I lived them one after another, but as I look back now, more than 20 years seem to have passed in no time at all. I am not sure when I stopped having nightmares of that sordid day you beat me and made me beg. Or when I stopped flinching when a man touched me, or when I stopped wincing whenever I met someone with your name. But some time in those 20 years, as I rebuilt my life with courage, filled it with happiness and hope for the future, I have freed myself from all that is you. I am my own woman. I shall continue to make my own way, at my own pace, however meandering the rest of this life may be.

I have forgiven you. Not for you, but for me.

AMY CHIA is a bossy daughter and sister, over-indulgent aunt, half-retired marketeer, rookie writer, (solo) wanderer, hopeless daydreamer, and an ever-faithful friend of the sea. She is working on a collection of travel flash fiction and will be starting a new adventure as a student in literary writing in 2022.

When Lovers Die (II)

Paul Rozario-Falcone

My Darling Aly,

I am thinking one morning of all the things you had said not to do. I have made this list while looking at life slowly waking up in the campo Santa Maria Formosa in Venice: Vegetable and fruit stands fully laden, but with hardly anyone buying at this hour. I keep scanning for little old ladies, thinking that where they shop, there will I shop too. Instead, there are lots of dogs, beautiful dogs, going about their business, people calling out to each other as they pass. Beautiful people. I am in a place of such beauty: Tall, slim bell towers, braggadocio, white linen, pistachio brioche, Tiepolo sky, and oh, such beautiful people. And yet the list of what not to do comes up:

1. Don't buy a house (in Italy); it is cheaper to rent.
2. Don't get hung up on a person; if they do not like you, move on.

3. Get over it (okay, this was what to do, as opposed to what
   not to do)
4. Don't do too much!
5. Don't think people are against you. That is just being silly.
   If only you could see yourself the way I do.
6. Get over it.
7. Like my mother, the one who had loved you like a son,
   once said: "Get over it!"

I wrote to a teacher the other day, saying it is terrible to
walk blind in a place of such beauty, thinking only of how few
people wear masks and how close we all are when crammed
into the narrow streets. I must say there is such a sense of
relief when I get to the edge of the island, where there is sky
and air and water. The narrow *calle* (streets) and *corte* (courts)
and *fondamente* (embankments) are just too full of people to
think of anything else. Or maybe it is just me, wandering
about in this daze of fear and sadness.

I suppose I asked for this, didn't I, Aly? I know just how
to make myself sad. I am here in Venice entirely because of
you. You had put the idea of my novel in my head. One day,
back in Singapore in lockdown in Braddell Heights, I was
minding my own business, trying to cook in the kitchen,
when all at once I spied this couple in the flat downstairs,
his semi-clothed body, hers wrapped in a black tank top,
both cooking together. And so, the story of Maestro and
Luca was born, Venetian artists in the mid-17th century.

Someone asks me what I am doing in Venice, and I
jokingly reply I am chasing ghosts. Only later does it dawn
on me how true this is. Although I think I am chasing the

ghosts of Luca, Maestro and the characters in my book, I am, in fact, chasing you, while you gracefully ascend to where you need to be.

One night, as I look for a map of Venice that I thought I had saved on my computer, I find instead your scanned pictures of a trip you had taken here in 1984. You had carefully labelled them. There you were, in your youth, with a healthy Jim by your side. Both beaming in a crowded Piazza San Marco, the basilica behind you. I panicked. I did not know what to think. I had found you in Venice, and I was devastated. I flipped through the handful of your Venice pictures, trying not to think too much. It was winter and cold, judging by how much fur people in the pictures were wearing. Or was fur just trendy for young bohemians at that time (your favourite Puccini opera)? I think I recognise one of the women in the pictures, Rosalba, in heavy dark fur. Her husband, Fabio, holds an infant, Elio, his firstborn. And Jim is towering over you.

I close the computer. I have found your beautiful, smiling face in Venice, and it is unbearable – the pain of experiencing your loss again, the pain of being in a place of such beauty without you. For all beauty loses meaning without you. All light grows dim without you, and I find myself sitting in the dark, numb. *Quando vedo te, vedo la luce (When I see you, I see the light),* a child once said to you. *E senza te, non c'è più la luce (And without you, there is no more light),* is what I say now. *Caro mio, tesoro mio, non so come vivere senza te. Sono distrutto. (My dear, my darling, I don't know how to live without you. I am destroyed.)*

Several mornings later, on my walk, I come across a piazza I recognise from your photographs. Piazza Santo Stefano, by the Accademia. I am reminded yet again of why Venice, why Luca and Maestro. Your weekly visits here from Bologna in 1971 to study art history. You always chuckled when you described your year abroad. The year Paul was born, you would say. We both got a kick out of attending medieval universities, and we each took the other to visit them. Oxford and Bologna, a union in Brooklyn. What a life, Alphonse, what a life. And then I walk to Piazza San Marco and take a picture in front of the incredible basilica, trying to recreate the one of you and Jim.

My Darling Aly, you would not believe how quiet these gondolas are when they glide by. I have been able to observe them from above as they navigate the intersection of rio de San Polo and rio di San Stin. Four canals head roughly north, south, east and west away from me. I can only really see the gondolas when they enter rio San Stin; they glide beneath my balcony. I see the wonder on the faces of children and adults. Warms my heart. I have a truly lovely perch here. Further east, gondolas glide under a bridge crisscrossed constantly by people. I listen to the lapping of the water against the sides of Venice. To be sad in a place of such beauty is doubly sad. The coolest looking people just power by in a boat, making the canal leap with lapping water. The sound is gorgeous – licking, slurping, completely sexual, and the cool people dressed for a day of seduction. This is the life you want me for me, not these tears that fall from the balcony into the pale, jade waters below. A man in a boat with a gorgeous dog in it. That is what you want for me, I know. A gorgeous Italian man who cooks for me and looks after me, just like you did. The peace of a gondola ride in the sun. The water is calm when nobody passes, always rippling though, rippling and reflecting the life above. These are just some of what you want for me.

My Darling Aly, my writing is like my grieving. It comes in waves. Like the water in the canals agitated by motorboats, my grief splashes about when triggered by a photograph of you or a memory of your brilliant smile. The reflection of the palazzo tries to form on the water. But ripples only allow colour and shape, no details yet. Occasionally amid the ripples, the windows can be seen, their white outlines, but the not the slenderness of their Byzantine curves and points. For that, the water must be calm. Writing is like waiting for calm, so that the image, once blurred in the ripples, can emerge. My writing, like my grieving, comes in fragments. A lady waits under the arch of a water entrance for a boat that has been double parked (double-moored?), wondering how she might board. Gondolas can pass each other within an inch without sideswiping. The voices of gondoliers explaining Venice in their various tongues. I wonder where, when not guided by a gondolier's oar, would a gondola wander. A couple plot their photographic moves on a *fondamenta*. They spy me.

Last night, or early this morning, I bit the inside of my right cheek so hard there was blood on my pillow. I had had a nightmare. I was in a city so terrifying, inhabited by beings whose only intent was to kill me. Faceless, nameless, except for two colours, black and red. And a singular form – sharp, metallic edges, like knives. Forms that slashed and sliced through air and matter and me.

A group of blonde girls are having a picnic on the *fondamenta*. So carefree and beautiful in their summer dresses. I have my coffee, my warmth, my nourishment. *Fondamenta* are like layers of icing, their edges white and then grey granite slabs. I adore how silently the gondolas glide by me, punctuated only by "Oiii", "Oh yeah" or "O-yay", the shouts that act like horns to signal arrival at corners. The brilliant white of a gull in the sun. The gulls when they swoop and curl and loop and purl are as silent at the gliding gondolas beneath them. The ripples of air they create we do not see, but only feel if they swoop near us. Exposed brick, reddish in places, but now mostly grey and beige from age and sun. Plaster-painted Venetian red, both bright and fading, cracked in places to reveal white marble. Brick on the ground/water floor, plaster and marble on the first floor, wooden terraces right at the top. Colours and textures change from top to bottom. Like a life growing upward and old from birth to death. Signs of interior lives through hanging laundry and funeral parlours. Even the dead are sent off by boat to the cemetery island of San Michele.

My writing, like my grieving, is pattern. I adore how silently the gondolas glide by. Wooden window frames, grey, flaking. Worn-down marble outer frames with mini pillars and lintels, and the whole thing topped by three curved domes, the middle one with a pointed tip. Oriental. So why shouldn't Luca, my character, be South Asian, or specifically from Kerala, or have mixed Indian, Ethiopian and Venetian blood? Look at Venice herself. She is not white, has never been. My father's house has many rooms, just like the palazzi all around me. A huge source of comfort. Rooms for everyone. Writing and grieving are like watching a gondola in the distance. It gets closer and closer to me, coming into perfect focus. At that point, it is intense, alive, pulsating. And then the current slowly takes it away from me, leaving me a little more healed than before.

My Darling Aly, remember that beautiful young couple who decided to spend a year sailing around the Mediterranean? Well, they have asked me to meet them so that I can sail with them into the Venetian lagoon. It would be incredibly beautiful, I think. But I would have to take a train and a bus to meet them. I would have to double-mask and be on edge the whole time. Is it worth it? I won't know, because I decided not to go, at least today. But I might be tempted to go tomorrow or the day after, if only to experience what sailing into the lagoon might be like. It might help my book, for Maestro leaves Venice for an island in the northern lagoon to escape the plague. I will see how I feel.

This young couple, they had come to your wake. They, and their whole gang of friends. It was beautiful to see so many people from all parts of your life, and my life there in Brooklyn, together. A beautiful, exhausting, blur. Even Heather from Perugia came. I burst out crying when I saw her. I could not believe it. She brought that happy period of our life straight into Cobble Hill funeral home. Who would have thought? We were so happy there, weren't we? Soaking up Italian lessons in this jewel of Umbria. I do not know what Italy means to me exactly, now that you are gone. You will be so proud I have started translating a text from Italian to English, something we both would have loved to do together. I am trying to make Italy my own. An Italy rooted in both your experiences, your family here and a place to which I connect in my own way. I am so glad I had the courage to come here in the middle of this cursed pandemic, so that I could grieve you here and feel what it is like to be alone in the places where we were once together. You know, I Zoomed with Rosalba the other day. I thought I would cry with her, but the exact opposite happened. We laughed and were so happy to see each other again. She gave me a bunch of titles to read on the history of Venetian theatre and told me to visit the Marciana, which I did. A few days later, I had *aperitivo* (aperitif) with Ariele and her family, and Piernicola. You had brought these people into my life, my Darling Alphonse. I now share the friendships you started more than 50 years ago. And what an amazing time I had with Piernicola. We drank and ate and took a road trip to Croatia. On his last night in Venice, I was so drunk I promised to buy him a house in Rome and he broke down in tears, saying no one had ever wanted to do anything like that for him. Days later, I am still a little fragile from this week of excess, my body still has not resolved my reflux, and I am regretting my alcohol-induced delusions of grandeur and generosity. Piernicola says that now that you have gone, I am *lo zio dall'America* (uncle from America). Funny isn't it, that I have become the link now between your American and Italian families? This brown, gay man who is contemplating a life here in Italy. We are planning a mini-reunion next year in Procida, the island *Nonna* (Grandmother) and Libby left. *Nonna* never returned, but Libby did. I miss both of you so much, and many times I have recalled the story of how *Nonna* would calm you when you were upset. And I, too, imagine you caressing my hand

and saying everything will be all right. The other day, I had a dream that you told me to play the lottery and gave me numbers. Piernicola bought Lotto tickets, but no luck. I know you want me to find love and happiness again, so I have come to an uneasy peace with the poem you wrote:

Sonnet 1
by Alphonse Falcone, December 30, 2017

When lovers die their love with them dies too.
Even famous loves must share this fate.
Though monuments recall their love, it's true
No passion can another emulate.
Love's scope is but confined to poets' ink
As less than shadow does to form compete
For as the flames of love in both hearts shrink
All warm light's clear refraction does retreat.
So love depends on creatures that have life
And follows rules of all biology
Although eternal love in Art is rife
Its true home only is theology
This is life's function we should most revere
Us Tabernacles of the love we share.

Thank you, Aly.

Your handsome and brilliant young lover, Paul

PAUL   ROZARIO-FALCONE   is   a   Singapore-born,
Brooklyn-based author. He was the co-founder of the
Singapore Literature Festival in New York and the Second
Saturdays reading series. He is currently pursuing a Masters
in Creative Writing, which involves working on a novel set in
17th century Venice and translating a contemporary Italian
memoir into English.

The Letter You Will Never Read

Adib Jalal

To my dear Mizah,

These are the words you will never read, but they are all I have to fill the gap you have left behind. It took a lot out of me to write these down, but it is the only way the words I want to say and thoughts I have for you can still find a home.

It has been hundreds of days since I had had to lay you down in your final resting place, and it appears time does not really heal grief but just changes its form. It still lingers, but I am no longer paralysed by it. I have been putting in the work to fulfil my promise to you I will find the courage to move forward, and I have been trying my best to reframe grief as an opportunity to grow and evolve. My therapist is proud of me for the work I have been putting in, and I think you would too. It is a difficult lesson to go through but in some ways, I am glad it is me who has to carry this pain instead of you.

I am wiser now to know that wishing you were still around, or hoping I could have another day with you, is not helpful but painful. But I will stay foolish enough to get hurt from missing you. I miss being able to share the most mundane and the most exciting parts of life with you. I miss the ease we had with each other and going through challenges together. I miss doing things with you, though it is the doing nothing I miss more. I miss the very idea of you. But most of all, I miss having you love me back.

From where I am today, it appears this is what life is all about: We live, we die, and in-between, we love. Or at least we try to figure it out. Some spend their lives looking for love; some try to make themselves worthy of love, and some become love. For me, I have spent a part of my life wondering if it even exists. But because of you, I know it does.

I still marvel at the fact we could have met each other much earlier in our lives but a higher power was delaying it to prepare us for each other. We were in the same architecture school, separated by just a couple of cohorts; but in a place where almost everyone knew one another, I did not even know you existed, although you knew I did. To think we might have walked past each other along the corridor or merely separated by a few seats in the lecture theatre, and yet our paths did not cross! Then, there was that time you had applied to be an intern at the design studio where I worked, and you saw me at my workstation. But, as fate would have it, you did not get the job and once again, we did not meet.

It must have been a cosmic nudge that led me to you, for I almost did not make it to the event where we first met. I was not feeling so great that day and was close to bailing out of visiting the mini-showcase which you were a part of, but decided to make a quick stop instead. That turned out to be where our paths would finally cross and begin intertwining.

I remember when I first met you, I thought of you as both a gentle flower and a brave lioness. And as I got to know you more, I learnt you were also made for grand ambitions and driven pursuits, just as much as cosy snuggles and slow Sundays. You never liked big gestures but you always wanted big things for others. Your heart was as beautiful as you looked. My heart easily became yours.

I never expected you to complete me in any way, and I certainly did not expect being with you would lead me to believe in love so much. You were the one who wanted to know the whole story of why I am the way I am. You were incredibly generous and tender with my flaws and shortcomings. You listened and supported me through my darkest struggles and brightest dreams. What more can the heart of a man desire? What more motivation does a man need to give everything and become his best self?

It did not take long for me, in fact for both of us, to know what we had was special. Everything just felt right and easy. After dating for a year, I proposed and you said yes. I wrote and read five simple sentences as my wedding vow to you. We promised we would grow old together, but we could not have known it was to be a promise life would not let us keep. I needed you for the rest of my life, but instead all I could have, was to be there for the rest of yours.

Sometimes, when I miss you, I would think of the early days of us figuring out living together under one roof.

Remember how I would get annoyed at you leaving multiple cups around the house? Or how you would get annoyed at my compulsive need to put things in order? It still puts a smile on my face when I think of how we would just laugh off this silliness.

I also remember how we looked at our meagre savings and decided we still had enough to splurge on a good dining table for the new house – because we would build our life together around it. You enjoyed your family dinners, while I grew up without much of it, and so we decided it would be the foundation of our shared life. We imagined – and actually did – hosting gatherings around it, with friends and family who would balm our hearts and fill it with joy. We also made a commitment to have dinner together at home as much as we could, and although it became more difficult as our work started to escalate, it was the one thing we would try the hardest to make happen.

It was also at that very dining table we discussed your career move that would define your legacy. I remember you telling me you thought of quitting your full-time job to dedicate your energy to Participate In Design, the non-profit design organisation you had co-founded. We had little savings, no security net, and were partly supporting our own families. I had just started my own company and was still trying to make the business work. To top it off, the organisation would not be able to pay you a salary for the next few months too. It was a crazy and an almost irresponsible thought to entertain, but in your voice was the conviction this was something you had to do. In your eyes was the glints of light you wanted to bring to others. The only right thing to do was to support you in every way I could.

To be honest, I envied your sense of purpose. You always seemed to know what you wanted to do with your life, and

I was just pleased I got to be a part of your successes. Sure, it was not all smooth and we had to sacrifice a lot, but I would do it all over again for you. All I ever wanted was to make you feel loved, heard and supported.

You cannot hear me tell you or show you I love you anymore, but I hope that having done it for every day we had been together counts for something. I know I will always remember you telling me you love me. I will always remember the words you would say to pick me up when I collapsed from the weight of the world I tried to carry on my shoulders. I will always remember the silence you calmed me with when the world got too noisy for me.

It took us a few years to get to a point where things seemed to be going right for us. Our careers were taking off, we were tasting comfort and rhythm in our lives, and we had the courage to think about the future. But then, it didn't. A seemingly innocuous stomach ache escalated to become a more serious concern that led me to rush you to the hospital in the middle of the night.

I have never told you this, but when we were in the A&E ward and I was pushing you on the wheelchair to the observation area, we passed by a huge infographic encouraging males to go for a colonoscopy. It stated that colon cancer was the number one cancer for men. I immediately thought: "Oh god, please do not let this stomach ache of hers be this."

But it was to be exactly it. It was a foreshadowing of your stage 4 colon cancer diagnosis.

I still remember your first words to me after you were diagnosed: "I'm sorry." You repeated those words again and again as you sobbed while our world collapsed. I could only hold you as I promised we would get through it together. I did not know how, but it was all I could do then. It was to be a promise I would repeat often and try to fulfil every single day from then on.

I hope your life was made a bit better by the exertions I put in in the years that followed. I was in a constant high-alert crisis mode as I shed almost all parts of my life to dedicate my capabilities, faculties and resources to caring for you. I could not control how fast the disease would consume you, so I tried to control everything else. If it could be researched and planned, I was on it. My head and notebook were filled with to-do lists, logistical arrangements, physical and mental care plans, meal and medication tracking, research papers, and all sorts of other resources. I worked even harder, I took on even more, and although I broke apart many times in-between, I made sure you never saw it. But you were so smart you probably would have known about it anyway.

I also could not tell you this before because I did not want you to feel bad, but I cried so much from seeing the chemotherapy and hospitalisation spells taking their toll on you. I made it my mission to support you with all I had, so you could enjoy one or two good days during the week to spend with family, friends or your life's work. Getting a glimpse of you out of the funk and glowing in your light was all I needed to keep on burning myself for you. I am glad you managed to enjoy quite a few of those in your last years. But actually, you were so graceful and brave throughout it all I sometimes wondered if you needed me at all. You were inspired and inspirational throughout the catastrophe; this will always be the image of you I will carry.

However, there was to be a time when your body broke down so much your spirit was shattered beyond repair. It was so difficult to see you in so much pain at the end and it was made worse by the fact I was not able to take it away from you. But you know what was the absolute worst? It was to look at your CT scans and lab results with the oncologist and realising the fight was over.

How do I look my wife in the eyes and tell her there is nothing more that can be done? How can I tell her she will most likely die in the next two weeks? How do I not kill her spirit before her actual passing? I will never know if I had delivered the bad news to you with enough gentleness and love, but I hope you know I did everything I could have possibly done from the day I gave you my heart.

It has been hundreds of days since you said your last words to me. I have had no choice but to find a way to live, and my life today looks nothing like what we had shared with each other. I think I have changed, and so has the world, but my love for you will not. Even though your ask of me was to fan the flames again, how can I ever be sure I am still capable of loving? Will there ever be someone who would risk her heart for me, and me for her? Maybe there is, maybe there isn't. All I know is there is a cemetery in every heart and your grave is in mine. All I can hear are the echoes of your love bouncing in the emptiness you left behind.

Forever yours,
Adib

ADIB JALAL is an urbanist who occasionally writes, and enjoys long walks. Mostly, his work involves building connections between people and place, and breaking down complex urban issues for discussion and action.

He was previously the director of placemaking studio Shophouse & Co where he co-created urban developments at various scales with a range of stakeholders. He also served as the Festival Director of *Archifest* in 2012 and 2013, and has held teaching positions at various tertiary design institutions. Adib also writes *Briefing of Urban Ideas* – a newsletter about cities – and *Dispatches* – a newsletter about walking, writing, and being. Find out more at adibjalal.com

OTHER BOOKS IN THE SERIES

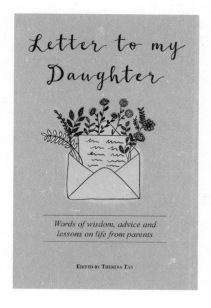

Featuring contributions by
Adlena Oh-Wong, Amy Poon, Ng Choong San,
Cynthia Chew, Dawn Lee, Dawn Sim, Janet Goh,
Jennifer Heng, Jenny Wee, Kalthum Ahmad, Karen
Tan, Landy Chua, Loretta Urquhart, Paige Parker,
Petrina Kow, Sangeeta Mulchand, Shaan Moledina-
Lim, Chiong Xiao Ting, Lin Xiuzhen, Yen Chua,
Zalina Gazali

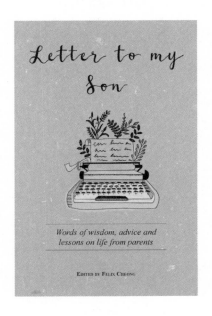

Letter to my Son

Words of wisdom, advice and lessons on life from parents

EDITED BY FELIX CHEONG

Featuring contributions by
Anitha Devi Pillai, Anthony Goh, P N Balji,
Bernard Harrison, Chris Henson, Christopher Ng,
Clement Mesanas, Daniel Yap, Darren Soh, Dinesh
Rai, Fong Hoe Fang, Gilbert Koh, Kenny Chan,
Lester Kok, Mark Laudi, Nizam Ismail, Olivier
Ahmad Castaignede, Roland Koh, Sanjay Kuttan,
Vicky Chong

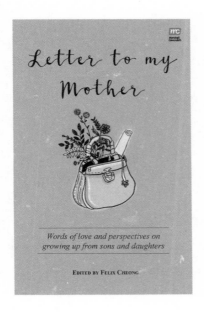

Words of love and perspectives on growing up from sons and daughters

EDITED BY FELIX CHEONG

Featuring contributions by
Christine Chia, Regina De Rozario, Tania De Rozario, Charmaine Deng, Nanny Eliana, Gwee Li Sui, Beverly Morata Grafton, Sharda Harrison, Lydia Kwa, Jo-Anne Lee, Faith Ng, Irene Ng, William Phuan, Martha Tara Lee, Rose Marie Sivam, Cheryl Charli Tan, Jean Tan, Wahid Al Mamun, Georgette Yu, Zuraidah Mohamed

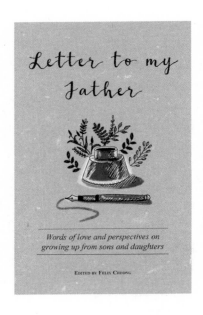

Words of love and perspectives on growing up from sons and daughters

EDITED BY FELIX CHEONG

Featuring contributions by
Margaret Thomas, Sadie-Jane Alexis Nunis,
Christina Thé, Louis Tong, Alvin Tan, David Kwee,
Hoh Chung Shih, Wong Ting Hway, Chee Soo Lian,
Natalie Ng, Charmaine Leung, Crispin Rodrigues,
Jacintha Abisheganaden, Kelvin Tan, Usha Pillai,
Andrew Koh, Patrick Sagaram, Loh Guan Liang,
Sarah Voon, Koh Jee Leong